Explorations in Group Work:
Essays in Theory and Practice

Explorations in Group Work: Essays in Theory and Practice

Edited by
SAUL BERNSTEIN

LOUISE A. FREY, JAMES A. GARLAND,
HUBERT E. JONES, RALPH L. KOLODNY,
LOUIS LOWY, MARGUERITE MEYER

Milford House Inc.
Boston

Library of Congress Cataloging in Publication Data
Main entry under title:

Explorations in group work.

    A project of the Group Work Theory Committee of
the Group Work Dept. of Boston University School
of Social Work.
    Includes bibliographies.
    CONTENTS: Frey, L. and Meyer, M. Exploration and
working agreement in two social work methods.--
Garland, J. A., Jones, H. E., and Kolodny, R. L. A
model for stages of development in social work groups.--
Bernstein, S. Conflict and group work. [etc.]
    1. Social group work--Addresses, essays, lectures.
I. Frey, Louise A. II. Bernstein, Saul, 1905-
ed. III. Boston University. School of Social Work.
Group Work Dept.
HV45.E94   361.4   73-9596
ISBN 0-87821-146-2

Published by Milford House Inc.
Publishers at 85 Newbury Street, Boston, Massachusetts 02116
Copyright© 1973 by Saul Bernstein
International Standard Book Number 0-87821-146-2
Library of Congress Catalog Card Number 73-9596

Printed in the United States of America

CONTENTS

PREFACE

To bemoan the state of theory in group work and in social work generally has become a popular and perhaps unhealthy pre-occupation. There is the temptation to throw out all that has been evolved, and to say or imply that a new theory day is dawning with one's own product, — a manifestly unfair and overly ambitious position. There is also the temptation to deplore the situation, to criticize what has been done by others and to stop there, on the assumption that someone else will carry the responsibility for moving the enterprise forward. A third temptation is to aim very high, to ask theory to be all-embracing and all-integrating, an impossible goal.

Nevertheless, the need for new theory is acute. It has appeal for those concerned with knowledge building for its own sake, but the concern here is for undergirding, enlightening, deepening and making more effective the services given to people in groups by social workers and others. Without good theory, the diagnosis and intervention by group workers tend to be hit or miss. While many excellent theory guidelines have been developed over the years, there are also gaping holes.

With thoughts such as these, the Group Work Department of the Boston University School of Social Work decided to devote time and energy (how much was not anticipated) to theory building. To round out the effort, representatives of casework, community organization and social psychology were invited to join what became the Group Work Theory Committee. Its members included a balance between practitioners and teachers.

As is typical of a new group, even though all the members knew each other well, there was much groping for a way into the task and for a framework. The meaning of theory was explored on a rather abstract level, and many specific theories were examined in relation to actual group work experiences and in general. Cross-referencing to casework, community organization and to social psychology was helpful.

Agreement was reached early about the goal of writing when our ideas might merit publication, giving us further incentive to push toward culmination. But the design for our efforts was not easily achieved. At least these approaches were considered:

1. Work on the theory building process, which was found helpful but not sufficient.
2. Focus on the theory gaps most acutely in need of attention. This criterion was respected but was not regarded as the sole determinant.
3. Select an over-all theme and subdivide it among us. The final decision was to accept some unifying ideas (see Introduction) but to allow for and even to encourage diversity in the specific subject matter. Without this diversity, the task could become mechanical and un-inspired.
4. Most of the Committee members had interests on which they were eager to work. In encouraging the pursuit of such interests, we thought that the chances for creativity and originality would be increased. The total enterprise and the criticism of the others to each article were taken seriously but the authors were given autonomy. We regarded it as part of our mores as a group to listen attentively while the author's production was criticised rigorously, but the writer's decision was final.

The work of the Committee began in 1959 and continued until 1962. Various circumstances delayed publication until 1965. This accounts for the absence of references to material published during the period 1962–65.

Many meetings and much individual work went into what follows. However it may be received, the members of the Group Work Theory Committee have already used the material in their practice, in teaching, in speeches, and in other ways. Our hope is that others will catch some of the flavor and substance of growth through reading it that the authors experienced in writing it.

Members of the Boston University Group Work Theory Committee:

Saul Bernstein, Chairman, Professor and Head of Group Work Department

Robert Chin, Research Associate, Human Relations Center and Professor of Psychology, Boston University

Donald Feldstein (briefly a member), Assistant Executive Director, Jewish Community Centers, St. Louis, Missouri

James Garland, Director of Activity Therapies, McLean Hospital, Belmont, Massachusetts

Louise Frey, Associate Professor, Group Work Department

Hubert Jones, Assistant Director, Roxbury Multi-Service Center

Ralph Kolodny, Director of Group Work Department, Boston Children's Service Association

Louis Lowy, Associate Professor, Group Work Department

John McDowell, Dean of School of Social Work

Marguerite Meyer, Community Project Developer, Worcester Youth Guidance Association

INTRODUCTION

Groups are fascinatingly and challengingly complex. Their attributes run almost the whole range of human interests and professions. Where to take hold, what is truly meaningful in terms of social work values and goals, where to sink the shaft of inquiry, are difficult questions. And yet the decision to move in one direction rather than in others carries with it long range commitments and consequences. It is something like digging a well. How accurately one can predict that there is water under the surface profoundly affects the outcome of what may be an enormous effort.

The possibilities are all too numerous: the color of the paint on the walls of the meeting room, the time of the day and of the year, the psychodynamic history of each of the members, the rise and fall of international crises, the rate of unemployment, the number of aggressive acts by the members, the stage of the groups development, how the group was formed, the handling of conflict, patterns of decision making — these and many other variables could be studied and theories could be developed about them. What guidelines are available for deciding where to take hold? This should not be a capricious decision. Intellectual adventuring has its risks.

Not only is there a bewildering array of variables as suggested above, but the potential approaches to theory building present difficult decisions. One could consider (as our Committee did) the nature of theory, the definition of constructs, concepts, principles and systems. Another question is whether there are organized steps through which theory building must go, or whether such orderly steps tend to be retroactively grafted onto what were really good hunches or insights. This kind of examination of theory was found to be a helpful orientation rather than the heart of our interests.

The demands of practice are paramount and the experience of the Group Work Theory Committee on the firing line helped to focus on issues which arise when group work is done thoughtfully. While it can be helpful to speculate on the higher levels of abstraction, one of our final tests was always whether our theorizing would increase the understanding of groups, thereby improving service to them.

The other extreme, a kind of theorizing which is too close to the ground and too concerned with limited details, also has its dangers. It is not apt to provide the leverage for new generalizations and perspectives. The level we sought might best be called middle range theory, concentrating on intervention by the worker who is serving "live" and not laboratory groups. We did not regard other approaches as useless or frivolous. We selected the ones which seemed to promise the greatest productivity for us.

A troublesome characteristic of much of group work theory is its global character, i.e. the tendency to deal with values and goals, the ends to which intervention efforts should be directed, without being specific enough about methods and techniques. Values and goals are crucial and there is no intent here to de-emphasize them. On the contrary, developing clearer and hopefully more effective methods enhances the dignity of values and goals by providing better ways of realizing them. Nor should one disregard or belittle the elements of art and intuition. They do — and always will — play a prominent and significant role in work with people. Recognizing the force of all this, there is still an acute need for the kind of theory which provides a framework for guiding the specific acts of intervention of the group worker. This function preserves an important aspect of theory, that of ordering phenomena into meaningful patterns so that the worker's understanding of group behavior is enriched and he achieves leverage for more enlightened intervention.

Another guide was the state of the literature and available theory. While the subject of each of the four articles in this book is mentioned in many publications, it was our judgment that they had not been sufficiently developed. As we perceived the needs of practice, this development could be richly applied in group work.

A further criterion was consistency with existing theory and with the values and goals of social work. If inconsistencies should arise, as they sometimes did, we felt an obligation to resolve them.

While theory and research are interrelated in many ways, we thought it wise not to impose upon ourselves the requirements and restrictions of research. In an informal manner, we used group work experience to suggest and to test ideas, but we thought that we would be freer to build theory if we did not have to stop with each idea to formulate a research design and to apply it to data. Available studies were considered and it is our hope that our ideas will be subjected to the tests of rigorous research, but we took the position that it is productive at times to rely on hard thinking and insights without always becoming involved in the painstaking and slow processes of research.

A final guideline arose out of the decision to allow and encourage each of us to tackle a subject of his own choosing. The chances for creative thinking are greater when one feels a spark of inspiration than when one has a subject assigned to him.

The above were our primary guides in selecting areas for theory development. Some further thoughts were operative. The conditions under which group work is and should be practised were given lively attention. There was, for example, the temptation of a "false face", meaning that agencies could lure members to their groups by offering pleasant recreational and social activities, while really wanting to provide educational-treatment experiences. Miss Frey and Miss Meyer deal with this issue in their article.

Groups might be formed casually, with members coming and going, or with no clear patterns in mind. Some implications for this practice grow out of the paper by Garland, Jones and Kolodny.

The unexamined assumption can easily be made, and often is, that conflict is negative and messy, and therefore that it should be avoided. The Bernstein article probes this assumption.

Decision making might be regarded as a way to get things done effectively, so that the group can be productive. The Lowy paper makes clear that what is learned by the members and internalized as an ongoing way of dealing with problems is more important than the quality of the decision itself, although the two need not be mutually exclusive and can actually reinforce each other.

Some more general comments about group work are in order. Along with having various other characteristics and functions, group work is viewed as having problem solving concerns and responsibilities. The range is great. The problems could include helping a boy to control his impulses, guiding a girl toward a more feminine identification, stimulating members to be less inhibited in their approach to activities and to each other, fostering a franker and more intelligent way of dealing with conflicts and of making decisions, developing leadership, and many others. While many of the problems have a pathological quality, often associated with deviance, others involve tasks which relatively healthy people face. Group work has much to offer the sick, the alienated and the deprived, but its functions and contributions are not limited to them. Prevention and promoting growth are also basic.

Group work, if it is to be given a chance to operate effectively, must be taken seriously and thoughtfully. This house has many rooms: how groups are formed, work loads, the size and character of meeting rooms, the quality and training of workers, the kinds of goals assumed or articulated, and a host of others. Especially important in the thinking of the Group Work Theory Committee is the relationship between the worker and the group. It is one of the central dynamics for change and for helping people. It has depth and continuity. It includes diagnosis, a thoughtful assessment of what is meaningful, and intervention.

The foregoing paragraph helps to set the stage for the clarification of a term used in the articles of this book, "social work groups". They are composed of members who are served by agencies, in contrast with laboratory groups formed for research purposes, and with such task-oriented groups as boards or staffs of agencies. Social work groups can be formed in many ways: through long standing friendships existing prior to their contact with the agency, according to interests, in relation to combinations of individuals whose interactions are likely to support treatment purposes, etc. While social work groups, like others, have tasks to perform, the primary emphasis is on the development of their members. "The play is the thing" only insofar as the "play" or task supports the primary developmental purposes.

A brute reality had to be faced by the Committee. Grand and integrating theory, in the Freudian style, is not feasible or available. A variety of disciplines have done research and have theorized about groups, and the results do not fit into a neat and integrated whole. Specific theories should not be inconsistent, but all helpful contributions should be welcomed and critically examined. We are in an era — which could prove to be permanent — when, rather than reaching the grandeur of an omni-explanation, it seems sounder and more productive to concentrate on valid building blocks, however incomplete they may be.

In all frankness, it should be added that the four articles in this book also do not fit into a neat and perfect integration pattern in relation to each other. Yet there is a flow of continuity. The beginning is how groups are started (Frey and Meyer), with concern for mutual exploration and a working agreement between the members and the agency. These processes dignify and give depth to the transaction, taking it out of the realm of the casual and the careless and setting the stage for the serious and substantial experiences which are to follow.

The group is then launched on its voyage. What should be the group worker's expectations of the stages through which it will go and the behavior and feelings characteristic of each? Are such matters even speculatively predictable? The Garland, Jones, and Kolodny paper deals with these issues.

Every group, to continue to exist and to move, must engage in certain processes of interaction. We have selected for attention and analysis two crucial ones: conflict (Bernstein) and decision-making (Lowy). If the content of all four articles is carefully followed in practice, our contention is that the prognosis for the group so treated is apt to be more favorable.

All through this book two themes are underlined and emphasized, whatever else may be under consideration. Diagnosis, the process of clarifying data in terms of significant variables, goals and values, is one. The other and related theme is the worker's intervention. Each article not only presents some theory but it also suggests what the worker can do with it, how the worker's intervention is specifically affected.

Saul Bernstein

Saul Bernstein
> Professor and Head of Group Work Department, Boston University School of Social Work
> Formerly on Faculty of New York School of Social Work
> Author of *Youth on the Streets,* Association Press, New York, 1964

Louise A. Frey
> Associate Professor, Boston University School of Social Work, Group Work Department
> Formerly Director of Demonstration Project on Group Work with the Handicapped, Community Council of Greater New York
> Formerly Head of Group Work, Yale Psychiatric Institute, New Haven

James A. Garland
> Director of Activity Therapies, McLean Hospital, Belmont, Massachusetts
> Faculty, Boston University School of Social Work
> Formerly Director of Camping and Research, Boston Children's Service Association
> Formerly Consultant to Children's Unit, Metropolitan State Hospital and to Worcester Child Guidance Center

Hubert E. Jones
> Assistant Director, Roxbury Multi-Service Center
> Faculty, Boston University School of Social Work
> Formerly Director of Group Work, Judge Baker Guidance Center, Newton Unit
> Formerly Group Worker, Boston Children's Service Association

Ralph L. Kolodny
> Director, Group Work Department, Boston Children's Service Association
> Faculty, Boston University School of Social Work
> Formerly Research Supervisor, Boston Children's Service Association

Louis Lowy
> Associate Professor, Group Work Department, and Chairman of the Social Welfare Sequence, Boston University School of Social Work
>
> Formerly Assistant Executive Director, Jewish Centers Association of Greater Boston
>
> Formerly Assistant Executive Director, Bridgeport Jewish Community Centers
>
> Author of *Adult Education and Group Work,* William Morrow & Company, New York, 1955

Marguerite Meyer
> Community Project Developer, Worcester Youth Guidance Association
>
> Formerly Associate Professor, Casework Department and Director of Field Work, Boston University School of Social Work

Chapter 1

EXPLORATION AND WORKING AGREEMENT IN TWO SOCIAL WORK METHODS*

Louise A. Frey and Marguerite Meyer

In social work practice it is casework which has most consistently utilized the technique of exploration and the setting of a
working agreement as part of its methodology. Group work,
although it is also based in a study, diagnosis and treatment framework, has not had a similar development. Casework, therefore, has
much to contribute to the attempt to identify and develop these
techniques in group work. We have found that there are similarities
and differences in these aspects of the two methods, but are not
ready to attempt comparison. Instead we shall present separate,
and not necessarily parallel, descriptions of exploration and working agreement in casework and group work. Before doing this,
however, we are able to make some general observations about the
coming together of an agency and a person interested in its service.
Basically this process is the merging of two social systems into a
pattern of interaction which is defined by the expectations of each
of the systems and the limitations of the circumstances under which
they come together. The establishment of a pattern which is
deemed appropriate comes about by a mutual exploration of their

---

*In 1959, when the authors did their first work on this paper, they were able
to find only passing references to exploration and working agreement in
casework literature and no references in group work writings. They have
since noted occasional use of these terms in articles and in conversation
among practitioners and educators. Our students and their supervisors in
settlements, centers, hospitals, and clinics have, at our suggestion, systemati-
cally approached this aspect of group work method and tested these ideas in
practice.

1

desires, objectives and responsibilities. A description of this process and how the social worker guides it, is our aim.

Casework

Exploration is usually referred to as the mutual beginning considerations between worker and client of the problem presented by the client and the service desired, the services the agency has to offer and whether they are appropriate for the client. The worker begins the study process here, and determines whether the client can be served in the agency or should be referred elsewhere. The client decides whether he wants to be helped in the way the agency will do it. The depth of exploration into the request for help is related to purpose, setting and function and eventuates in a working agreement in which it is made clear how worker and client will proceed together in this relationship.

In the practice of casework, initial exploration which leads to the establishment of a working agreement for help between worker and client, has been recognized as an integral part of treatment. Exploration is conceived of as an enabling process which is done "with" the client, not "to" him. It opens up the client's problem as well as his and the worker's understanding of it in order that some action may be taken to relieve or modify the difficulty.

A client understandably approaches help with mixed feelings of both wanting and not wanting assistance. It is never easy to ask anyone for anything and no matter how great the need, there are trepidations and fears as well as longing to receive. These ambivalent feelings may be cloaked in various ways and presented in differing emotional forms. One client may show anger and demand his rights; another may appear humble and self-effacing; another may seem calm and unconcerned, or depressed and scarcely able to say anything.

The initial request for help may represent the actual need or it may be only a part of the real problem. It may, in fact, have nothing to do with the true concern. What a person is able to verbalize about his needs at the outset depends upon many factors of time, place, problem, and the person himself. People usually come for help at a time of crisis. Under the circumstances of such heightened emotion there may be a natural distortion of facts which causes some to present their needs not only in dramatic ways but also in unusual ones. Others, feeling the enormity of their problems,

2

may have to minimize or partialize them because they so greatly fear facing the full implications. Some may be so afraid of rejection by the agency that they ask for only part of what they want. Others may try to make the kind of request that they think is appropriate for a certain agency. Still others may not actually know what they want and request the first thing that comes to mind. Some people have greater understanding of themselves and are, therefore, able to ask for what they truly need. Some clients are not very adept at language because of their personalities, their ages, or educational levels so that their requests are articulated with a great difficulty. Children will often make their requests through non-verbal means.

The process of exploration is designed to take into account all of these variable emotions and forms of request. Acceptance of the feelings of the client, however these are made manifest, is strengthened by the way in which the interview is directed toward finding out what is troubling the person. Such direction relieves anxiety through bringing out into the open the client's awareness of the true nature of his difficulty. It makes use of the available feeling of the client and mobilizes his strength to face his problems as realistically as he can. In the context of the casework relation-ship which is in process of being established, the client is helped to determine the significance and meaning of his problem to him. The client who requested what he actually wanted is able to con-solidate this need. The client who requested part of what he wanted is gradually helped to see the fuller implications of his problem. The client who asked for something he didn't want is slowly enabled to discover his true dilemma.

Initial exploration, depending on the particular person and the nature of the problem, may require several interviews. The essence of each interview, in which exploration has been skilfully done, is that of togetherness. The caseworker carefully and thoughtfully proceeding at the client's pace, helps him bring out his concerns. Questions are asked and comments made that build on his own way of revealing his story. The caseworker supports him in his efforts to understand his own concerns and is respectful of the particular style he uses to accomplish this end. The applicant is gently brought back to the context of what he is saying only if his interpolations are truly leading him away from the essence of what he is trying to bring out.

The verbal and tacit understanding of the client's difficulty achieved during the stages of the initial exploration leads to a point of clarity from which the next step may be taken. The caseworker gives his professional opinion (based upon the psycho-social study) on the individual's need for help. He clarifies whether help is, or is not, possible with the problem and further, whether such assistance is available in this or another agency.

In the event that help is needed and it is appropriate for it to be given by the agency in question, the caseworker establishes this fact. It does not necessarily follow that because a person knows that he has a problem, he wants help with it. The helping process must take the direction of enabling the applicant to consider accepting assistance. The caseworker explores his expectations of help, particularly as they relate to this agency and follow him as he considers the pros and cons of his decision. The caseworker presents the reality of what help may mean (insofar as ascertainable) particularly emphasizing the way the services of this agency are given. Though the caseworker clearly supports the person's acceptance of help, he is encouraged to express his doubts. Questions are answered and misconceptions cleared up.

The eventual decision to use help leads to the working agreement. Throughout the process of exploration, the applicant has been experiencing the caseworker's methods and has become aware of the quality of the relationship which is here available to him. The caseworker has demonstrated an ability to respect a person and to value his feelings and has made clear the agency expectations that he will participate in helping himself. The applicant discovers that even though he may have learned no new facts about his problem, he now sees it in a somewhat different perspective. He has a sense of comfort in having shared his burden and takes some measure of reassurance from the fact that he can do something about his situation. He has, also, some feeling of accomplishment in having taken the first step toward a solution. Some of these feelings have been experienced rather than talked about and represent the non-verbal components of the working agreement. Exploration thus is enormously supportive as the individual anticipates the future of help for he has seen the caseworker's dedication as a professional person to help him and he knows he wants to be helped with a specified problem. Still unknown are what the future ramifications of that problem may prove to be, the precise goal to be achieved in regard to it, and the exact length of time it will take to accomplish it. Although the specific nature of the helping process is still unknown, enough of it has been experienced to be reassuring. Also supportive to the client is information about the practical details of help, the time and length of appointments, the place of meeting and the fee if there is one.

The working agreement is an integral part of treatment. It is the culmination of the initial exploratory period and enables the client to participate in a plan to use help in a way which substantiates his own decision for help and thereby implements his use of it. The working agreement may culminate initial exploration but it does not terminate it. Receiving help is a much too complex human experience to believe that the making of a working agreement resolves the ambivalences or the resistances to working on it. Exploration goes on throughout later stages of treatment, and greater understanding of a problem may require a revised working agreement. It is significant and characteristic of the whole process of casework which is based upon self help that its starting point is a clear decision made by an individual to avail himself of help which is exemplified in the working agreement.

Group Work

The process of arriving at a working agreement is no less complex in group work than in casework. The fact that exploration must encompass both the group and individual, and that settings in which some group work services are given are multi-functional, complicates the process considerably. Nevertheless, it is possible to identify elements of exploration in the early stages of this social work method. These are more easily seen in groups with clear foci, it is difficult to do so in groups with vaguer purposes. This seems logical enough if one follows the reasoning used in casework that exploration of a client's request for help is centered in a felt and troubling need which *must* be clarified for treatment to proceed further. This necessity for identifying the need probably stimulated the invention of exploration in casework; so too in group work.

In casework exploration is part of a treatment process. Does this mean that exploration applies only to treatment groups? It would seem not. The crucial determinant of whether or not exploration is a part of the group work method, is not a treatment focus, but rather the degree of clarity of purpose as stated by the agency and understood by the group members. In other words, if the agency is clear about its purposes in offering various kinds of group work services and if it believes that people have the right to know the agency's intentions before committing themselves to involvement, it will have to explore the applicant's reactions to these objectives, be they treatment or not, as well as his desires and expectations of group membership. It will not wear a "false face" but will present itself as the social work agency which it is.

Exploration begins at the point of application when the agency first learns of the request for service or membership. The request may be a simple expression of a common human need for social experience or it may have much deeper meaning. This will not be known however, until there is some communication about the request between the applicant and the agency worker.

Certainly the verbalized request to become a member of a group served by an agency is a socially positive one. There may be no sense of urgency, no desire to be helped with an unresolved problem, or if there is a problem, no awareness that the agency has an interest in helping or a particular competence to do so. Under such circumstances, what is to be explored? The answer is obvious: the membership request and the agency's offerings.

To explore such a request, it is first necessary to understand what membership is and how it fits into the idea of social work as a service. Bertha Reynolds in *Social Work and Social Living (1951)* gave ample evidence of the dignity and meaning of social service in a membership organization. She points out the danger to social work of the misuse of the term client, a word which originally described a class of dependents who sought the protection of patrician families. The dictionary today still maintains "dependent" in its definitions and adds "a user of the services of a professional". . . . Miss Reynolds's book expresses the concern that viewing people mainly as clients is a signal that social work may easily lose sight of the fact that people have a right to a responsible voice about the services they use. Perhaps another way of putting this is that as social work gains greater technical proficiency it is ever more difficult to avoid the pitfall of equating specialized knowledge and skill with superiority of status or wisdom in relation to the user of a service. Serving and being served is a relationship of mutual interaction of dependence, need and help.

6

The membership concept is one which provides a guard against the pitfall and provides, uniquely perhaps, in group service agencies an excellent way of actualizing some of social work's most precious values and beliefs. A member is one of the persons who compose a society, community or party; a member is part of the whole. This vitality of interconnection and sharing in the life of the whole, is an asset to group work services which unfortunately has not been fully appreciated either philosophically or practically. Its dignity has not been explicitly nurtured so that the process of joining an agency has been treated as an event of little significance for both the joiner and the joined. An absence of exploration into a request to join, demeans the agency program as well as the applicant, for it seems to say that the agency offers nothing of value to impart to the applicant. The applicant would not have the good sense to want to join the agency if he knew what it, as a social serivce, was set up to do for him.

When a casual approach to the period of application is replaced by a carefully, thoughtfully planned one, the exploration of the meaning of joining can be the beginning of a rich association between the member and the social workers in the agency. A frank recognition of the aspects of joining a social agency which are different from joining a social organization is an obligation of the agency toward its members which is not only philosophically sound but also eminently sensible and necessary to the growth producing experiences which are the concern of social work.

Perhaps examples will help to make the foregoing ideas clearer. These examples are not fragments of the imagination but are based in the reality of practice.

Registration at the Happy Corner Community Center finds a hundred children signing up for activities or for a "club". Parents are not in evidence unless they happen to come along. When they do come they are welcomed and assist the worker with registration of the child. Shortly after registration the children are distributed throughout the program in clubs, activity groups, and gym programs. Some who are known from previous years as having special difficulties, are placed more selectively, and everyone hopes for the best. When troubles do show up later among new children, the trained worker becomes engaged with the child to learn if the problem stems from a poor group placement or from some other aspect of the child's life. If he learns that the difficulty is not in the group, then the family situation has to come in for consideration.

Meeting a parent *after* a problem has arisen is not of course the best way of trying to be helpful.

In this example, there has been no coming to an understanding of the meaning and intent of the agency services; there has been no real decision on the part of the parents to be part of these services; there has been no professional relationship initiated. As far as the child and parents are concerned, all that occurred was a simple joining of a social organization offering leisure time activities. Help was not bargained for in making the commitment to membership, and help is not wanted now. The staff of the agency explains this unwillingness to consider the problem as typical of the "hard to reach" in the neighborhood and it does not look at its own practices to see if these had any part to play in the impasse between itself and some of its "members".

At the Sarah Hollingsworth Settlement House things are different. The initial period of a person's membership is planned as a two-step process of application and intake within which the applicant's expectations and agency services are explored. Children under the age of fourteen join not as individuals but as part of a family. Such membership requires interviews not just with the child but with the parents. In these interviews the intake worker identifies himself as a social worker and describes the various aspects of the agency program, such as the recreational activities, the group work service, the social action projects. If the parents decide they do not want to be involved in any aspect of these offerings, this right is respected. If they decide they do want their children to have experiences which will help them with their social development, bring out their potentialities, identify problems which may be worked on in the settlements or be referred elsewhere, the agency then moves into the next phase of intake in which information is gathered from the child and his parents, his interests, current and past group associations, his health and behavior, the process of his growth and development. Certain facts about the familial and social situation will give clues to the family health and needs. The intake worker at the Sarah Hollingsworth House finds that many parents voluntarily disclose their concern with family problems or their children's behavior, or they will ask questions about the school or about public assistance. This agency feels that this communication takes place because of the way it has presented itself as a social work organization.

The information gathered from the parents and an interview with the child is used to make the proper group assignment for the child and it paves the way for future contacts with the family, not only around problems, but around the strengths and potentials of the child. It makes it easier for parents to participate in programs designed to meet their needs for pleasure, education or assistance, and a program designed for the improvement of the community. Trust and respect have begun and will provide the base for future association.

In its teenage program, the Sarah Hollingsworth House realistically faces the fact that new adolescents will not come to its doors if families are to be involved in the membership process. It also accepts the fact that most teenagers do not want to be "improved" other than in dancing, basketball or other skills. The agency offers programs which do appeal to the teenagers and meet some of their very important needs, but it does not hide the fact that it has social workers on its staff and that if anyone has any trouble or problems, it is ready to help. It does not shortcut the application process but skilfully does it in a way which shows respect for the teenagers' interests by giving him the right to choose among its program offerings, and by telling him what the agency's expectations are for his part in the utilization of its services. Teenagers often apply to the settlement for membership as a group. A group intake which is based on the same principles, offers the worker an additional opportunity to observe some of the group behavior of applicants. The workers at Sarah Hollingsworth find this most helpful in deciding which worker is to be assigned to the group. When an intake is done with a group, the members are faced immediately with the fact that they will have to contend with an adult leader, advisor, or worker. They will not have to explore what being in a group may mean to them because they are already in one and ostensibly satisfied with it, but the intake worker asks them to begin to wonder about what the presence of an agency representative is going to mean to them. Although this is largely an intellectual matter to the group at this point, the assigned worker finds it of inestimable value when he and the group finally do come together in the early meetings.

The latter example has been presented to show how the beginnings of exploration and working agreement are made in the period before the first meeting of a worker with a group of people who have joined a social agency in order to participate in its program. We will later describe the intake stage in social work groups which are not in the setting of a membership organization or which have not made a request to receive group work services.

In group settings as well as casework, there are many people who did not originally request help, but who are receiving it. The agency in some cases has reached out to these people. In prisons or hospitals some are required to participate in the service. Street gangs are a classic target of the agency which reaches out. Certainly in the initial stages exploration is not likely to include individual interviews and the accumulation and assessment of family and social data. In such work, exploration has to be done by the agency, first to locate the clients with the problems with which the agency is concerned. Once the worker has found the gang, then it is his job to demonstrate to the gang what the agency has to offer them. Curiosity pushes the gang to inquiry; responsibility requires the worker to inform. In much of the literature on detached group work, the importance of honesty at this point to later success with the group is stressed. When the worker has tangibly demonstrated his interest in the members, and his understanding of their lives and feelings, more personal data about family and life history are voluntarily offered by many young people. Some may have to wait for crises in which they strongly feel the need for help to give the worker more of the background information. In such groups composed on non-trusting, suspicious youth, exploration inevitably goes on for extended and varying lengths of time at the group and individual levels, with most of the specifics of time, availability, etc. probably agreed upon before the exploration is finished.

Another population to which the group worker reaches out is patients in a hospital. It is common practice in hospitals to search out individually those patients with special needs in order to assign them to groups. Less usual is the approach to a ward group in which the aim is to intervene in the on-going daily group processes in order to guide them toward therapeutic ends or at least to prevent them from being anti-therapeutic. In these instances the population may not feel a pressing need for help with problems of group living and may not want if after it is offered. In the mental hospital, the patients may not be permitted a choice about participation, or they may be so disoriented that they seem unable to make a choice. Despite these obstacles, exploration proceeds apace and the working agreement with its verbal and non-verbal elements is eventually achieved. The pathology of the patients may slow down the pace and disarrange the sequence but nevertheless for treatment to have a possibility of being effective the approach-avoidance of this stage must be enjoined.

In a public school setting, one also finds people in need of service who may not want it. The example we shall give shows how initial exploration at intake was successful in eliciting a decision to receive a service, but how at the next stage of the actual reality of the group the emotional level of the challenge of participation resulted in a flight from help.

When Mrs. B. was approached by a social worker as a result of a teacher's referral of her child to the school social work department for group work experience, her initial response was that her child had no real problems although she was shy. She agreed that most children need to learn to get along better with peers and thought that her Ellen would enjoy being in a group and doing things. Further exploration had the mother saying she was worried about her child being so good. By the end of the interview, the mother said that Ellen's tendency to whine and her fearfulness in presence of the mother was both a source of annoyance and worry to her and she wondered if she had done anything wrong in raising the child. This beginning exploration during intake thus opened the possibility of further work with a mother of a child who was "too good".

The pre-group intake interview with Ellen explored her interests, her achievement in school and her friendships. Interests and friends were limited, although grades were excellent. Her timidity during the interview was broken only in one moment of daring when she said she wasn't sure she would like to be in a group. She presented these feelings only in a most constricted way and after further discussion said she would be willing to try out the group with the worker.

The next phase of exploration came when the children met one another. The character of the combination of these individuals was certainly not precisely predictable by the worker. It was an even greater unknown to the members of the formed group.

For Ellen, this first meeting confirmed her fears about being in the group. Her doubts became a certainty when she saw all the other group members. She was quiet during the meeting and worked a tight symetrical design with crayon. She told her mother she did not want to be in the group. When Mrs. B. tried to convince her she should not give up so soon, she began to scream that she would not be in a group with "stupid crazy kids". Her panic reaction affected the mother, who next morning rushed to the principal's office and denied that anything was wrong with her child and blamed the social work department for stirring up trouble in her home. Mother and daughter withdrew from help despite all efforts of the social workers to explore further and clarify the situation.

In this distressing example is seen the additional dimension which exploration has in group work, that of peers whose measure must be taken by the individual who is trying to decide if he wants to belong to the group. The real decision to affiliate comes only after the individual has actually experienced the other members.

Most people do not retreat in flight and panic from other group members as did Ellen in the example, but some reluctance to become significantly involved with others is certainly present in the beginning of most human relationships. Capacities for involvement and fears about affiliation naturally vary considerably with individuals, and similarly go with natural friendship groups which have to make a decision about whether they will become affiliated with the agency and its workers.

This ambivalence about closeness which is described in the next article in this book has to be worked through by exploring the nature of the new experience. In a new group the members study each other to find kindred spirits, to locate "enemies", to find a position and role in an emerging structure. They explore the social field to decide whether they want a place in it (for whatever needs, healthy or otherwise, it might possibly meet for them). Not only do the members in newly formed groups have to find out about each other, but they also have to find out about the worker (who has an advantage over them in knowing everyone in the group) and the agency. The members try to find out what the worker is like, where he sets limits, whether he likes and approves of them, whether he will give to them, understand them, be fair, whether he can be trusted. This is where members of natural groups place their energies rather than in each other. Following is a specific illustration of exploration by a child in a group, newly formed of children in two grades in the same public school.

Debby, who was living in a foster home and who had had to go to a special school the previous year, said in an intake interview that she'd like to be in a group because she had no girl friends. During the first group meeting she openly expressed her fright about hurting herself and to show considerable concern about the members breaking the equipment in the room. For three weeks this behavior was repeated until she saw that she was safe in the club. She observed that the worker would not allow destruction of the classroom and that the worker stood by to help her literally to keep her balance. When she tested the worker's interest in her a few weeks later by announcing she had to quit the club to go to Scouts with her sister, she found that the worker wanted her to stay, and the next week, she announced that she didn't have to go to Scouts. At this point she seemed to commit herself to involvement in this relationship and in the next few meetings she played *with* another girl at the doll house, saying to the worker, "I usually don't play with someone else". The week after, she quietly contributed the information to the group that she had been in a special class once. (In her interview with the group worker, she had told her that this was the one thing in her life she'd like to forget). The following week, when the group was making recordings of their voices, she said into the microphone that she was "adopted" and listed the names of her adopted family and real family. (The real truth about her families did not come until the end of the year in another stage of group development). Then for the first time she played freely and noisily with two girls, and she lingered behind with several others to "help" the worker clean up.

From this point on it was fairly clear that she had done enough exploration to satisfy herself that she need not be afraid and inhibited in the group. Enough trust had been established for her to come closer to the others and the worker than was customary for her. The others had gone through a similar process and arrived at a decision to affiliate at different times. Each and all were assisted in their exploration by the worker's activities. .

While Debby was exploring her new situation – its dangers and promises – the worker was observing her behavior, her fears, and her skills. This observation gave the worker the information she needed to intervene appropriately in order to relieve anxiety, provide physical and psychic support and protection, and help her to resolve her ambivalent feelings about being in the club. The worker demonstrated that she cared whether Debby came to the club each week or quit. Much of the worker's exploration was non-verbal and was accomplished through use of program media and manipulation of the environment. For example, the doll house was set up because of Debbie's interest in it, but two chairs were placed in front of it so that someone would sit next to Debby in the hope that parallel play would become interactive. Through this non-verbal action, the worker gave the child an opportunity to relate safely and successfully to another child in the group and decrease her anxiety and ambivalence about being in the group. The child's statement that she usually played alone verbalized the loneliness that was one of her problems, and was related to her understanding of the purpose of the group: to help children make friends.

In general, the worker's exploration activities consist of making observation of the behavior of the members as individuals and as a potential group and giving members a chance to observe him from a safe distance. He offers activities which maintain the distance but which also provide bridges to closeness when the members are ready to use them. Activities open opportunities for further exploration of social capacities, frustration tolerance, controls, interests, skills. He verbalizes the obvious and ambivalent feelings and reservations about the group and gives permission for this study period to take place by not requiring commitment or a degree of involvement beyond each member's readiness. The testing so often referred to in our literature is accepted by the worker as the members' right to guard themselves in a new situation. His permissive, but limiting, protective, but enabling stance presents to the members an identifiable stable person about whom a decision can be made. The decision, of course, is whether to invest self in the group in the worker, and the agency.

The decision to become affiliated with the other people in the group is not just a matter of liking or disliking them. In a social work group the struggle with accepting the stated purpose is tied in with the decision about future close association with the people. As the purpose grows clearer, the working agreement becomes firmer. The worker's behavior as he helps members through the initial stage of the group sets the framework of the working agreement. The worker articulates the specific terms of the agency service as applied in this group and elicits members' reactions and feelings, both behaviorally and verbally. The verbal adult group can be helped to verbalize, the non-verbal group may need worker's clarification of evident feelings and responses. The working agreement is established as group and worker recognize why they are together and what is expected of each in this relationship.

The working agreement becomes a reference point throughout the group life and is a dynamic force in accomplishing its objectives. This clear understanding of purpose is an important foundation for the development and maintenance of trust. Members should not be tricked into involvement under false pretenses if a helping relationship is to be established. The group which is not clear about its purposes and the working agreement can use this obscurity of purpose as a means of resisting deeper evaluation, greater self-awareness, and full responsbility. Handling such resistance is much more difficult for the worker who may or not be sure himself of what his and the agency's goals are. With those members in whom mistrust is a significant personality dynamic, the working agreement can be a source of reassurance and a damper on delusional ideas. To the "normal" person the working agreement expresses respect for him and helps him engage in a responsible way in the group experience.

The working agreement as indicated earlier is also significant in the work with parents of children who are members. A parent's consent and understanding is certainly necessary if a child is to participate in group experiences which group workers'claim are so potentially significant to his development. Again, this is related to social work's central belief in the right of the individual to choices freely made upon consideration of the issues and alternatives. It is vital in helping the parent overcome resistance when a problem about his child has to be brought to his attention for further treatment or referral.

Exploration leading to the establishment of a working agreement is a dynamic force in the group. It should be noted here that there is no definite time table for this aspect of the method. In one sense there is continuous exploration and the renewal of the agreement in work with a group. However, the beginning phases of the method have a particular use to make of this technique of exploration, and the suggestion is made here that this conceptualization will not only make this phase and subsequent ones more meaningful to those being served, but will help crystallize social group work practice as it has done in casework.

Conclusion

We have only begun to suggest some of the ways in which the social worker guides the exploratory process in group work and casework. In both methods the workers receive their basic direction from the objectives and values of the profession, from the principles which stem from values and knowledge. It would seem that the process of helping people arrive at decisions to accept or reject services based upon a clear understanding of its terms and implications, is a tangible expression of the philosophy fundamental to social work. As such this process deserves greater attention than it usually receives; as a practical method of soundly merging agency and client into an interaction which is designed to enhance the latter's social functioning, relieve his suffering, treat his ills, restore him to himself and the community, or anyone of the many other objectives of social work services. Such clear identification not only improves our helping methods but also makes the process easier to teach, to learn and to practice. Time spent in refinement of techniques is justifiable only when it results in more effective service to people. There is evidence to support our belief that in this instance this is true. We look forward to the enrichment and improvement by further practice of these ideas about process of exploration and the establishment of the working agreement.

Chapter 2

A MODEL FOR STAGES OF DEVELOPMENT IN SOCIAL WORK GROUPS*

James A. Garland, Hubert E. Jones, Ralph L. Kolodny

I. INTRODUCTION

Practitioners of social group work are continually faced with the question of group development. Virtually from the moment members enter the front door of an agency, the group worker begins his assessment of "Where the group is". With whatever means he has at hand, he tries to evaluate the core problem with which members are struggling, their needs and capabilities as individuals and as aggregates and their state of readiness for the acceptance of particular forms of service from the agency. Once having considered where the group or individual is, however, workers tend to devote little attention to a systematic examination of "where they go" and studies of on-going practice with a particular group rarely include a methodical investigation of the steps in the group's evolution. Our practice discussions generally stress the diagnosis of single events, their short-range emotional impact or long-range organizational effects, and the development of technical agility on the part of the worker in meeting crises in interaction. We have not given enough attention to the possibility that there are definable

*The authors are deeply indebted to their former colleague, Miss Virginia Burns and their former research consultant the late Samuel Waldfogel, Ph.D., both of whom played an important part in the original conceptualization of the model. Thanks are due also to Mlles. Corrine H. Carr and Carol A. Jenkinson and Mr. Robert Paradise, Department colleagues, who participated actively in the elaboration and testing of the ideas presented in this paper.

17

phases through which groups pass in the course of their existence. Nor have we considered sufficiently the likelihood that the identication of such phases may have important implications for the understanding of member behavior and the activity required of the worker in order to handle it appropriately.

When we are questioned as to the causes of a particular event in the life of a group or asked to decide among alternatives for action in dealing with it, our responses do indicate that we have an appreciation that the same behavior at different points in a group's experience may have different meanings and accordingly should be responded to differently. Also, we do explain member's reactions in terms of whether they are just starting the group experience or terminating it, or have been together for some time. In this sense, we are operating on the basis of at least a crude theory of developmental stages. Our tendency here, however, is to concentrate on the behavior displayed by members as they enter and then, much later as they finally leave a group experience. The long span between the group's birth and its dissolution seems to be seen theoretically as a rather undifferentiated period during which a number of occurances, problems, crises, satisfactions and shifts in relationships, can occur at random. It is significant in this regard that the bulk of direct practice that is done in the field – and, consequently, the bulk of material available for analysis – is performed by social work students and untrained part-time and volunteer leaders. Given the anxieties around controls and establishing an initial group contact that the neophyte leader typically experiences, and the fact that treatment time is governed more by academic and program years than by therapeutic design, it is not surprising that we have focused most of our attention on beginnings and endings. Where middle phases start to develop they are usually cut short by the leader's graduation or planning for summer camp.

Only occasionally is there an indication in the group work literature that there may be a sequence or order of development in a group's growth toward social maturity, during the substantial period between formation and termination.[1] It is rarely suggested,

[1] Kindlesperger, Walter. "Stages of Group Development", *The Use of the Group in Social Welfare Settings,* (mimeographed) Tulane University School of Social Work, New Orleans, 1957, pp. 8–9 and Northen, Helen, "Social Group Work: A Tool for Changing Behavior of Disturbed Acting-Out Adolescents", in *Social Work with Groups,* 1958, New York: National Association of Social Workers, 1958.

furthermore, that the stages in this sequence may be identifiable, and that there may be a relationship between the behavior displayed by members and the group's stage of development at the time that the behavior occurs. Even where there is reference to various stages, the emotional significance of each of them remains but little explored and indices of a group's movement from one stage to another are generally lacking.

It is now commonly accepted that individual human beings must work through a series of problems in the source of their development and that each of these problems in turn will demand certain psychic energies more than others at particular times of his life. For every child at one age it is his relationship to the parent of the same sex, at another, his independence from the family, and so on. In trying to understand the behavior of our groups as entities, group workers, perhaps out of concern that they not be accused of thinking of the group as an organism, have rarely explored the possibility that our groups, too, have to contend progressively with specific relational problems in a particular sequence as they continue to meet. Our failure to explore this possibility more assidously not only could be cutting us off from additional theoretical knowledge but may handicap us as we seek to evaluate and respond to the behavioral phenomena we encounter.[2]

What we require is a longitudinal understanding of group life. The task that confronts us is to identify and describe the kinds of problems that typically arise and the sequence in which they occur as groups continue to meet and evolve patterns of action and interaction. If we can conceptualize levels of development which those problem areas represent we shall be better able to anticipate and respond to behavior in a way that is appropriate to its developmental context. Awareness of developmental stages will provide workers with a framework within which to judge when action is needed to help a group to deal with and overcome an obstacle to its growth. In addition to possibly speeding up development,

---

[2] Chin's observation on this matter may be of particular interest to group workers. He is among the most recent of the social psychologists who have emphasized and outlined the value of developmental models for practitioners interested in any form of planned change. Chin, Robert. "The Utility of System Models and Developmental Models for Practitioners", *The Planning of Change,* Bennis, Warren G., Kenneth D. Benne and Robert Chin, Ed., New York: Holt, Rinehart and Winston, 1961.

knowledge of a group life-pattern may provide a better basis for determining when a group had done all it can in aiding the social and emotional growth of its members and should be terminated. A group developmental theory demands that we pay close attention to the core problems with which the individual must cope in entering into and maintaining himself in relationships in small groups. As a result, concern with such a theory may lead us to take a second look at the characteristic relationships between groups and the agencies of which they are a apart, and especially at the tasks which the former are expected to accomplish as agency units. It may very well be, for example, that groups, even those made up of rather stable members, are too often called upon to participate in agency-wide projects as well-functioning units before members have had an opportunity to master the relational problems they encounter in simply coming together and staying together as a group. Finally, it is also hoped that the stage-problem construct may be employed as a testing device against which individual personalities and reactive patterns may be diagnosed and evaluated.

II. THE STATE OF OUR KNOWLEDGE

Group workers have not usually devoted a great deal of their professional effort to conceptualizing their ideas on development *per se.* However, leading workers in the field have touched on the theme as they have drawn, in broad outline, systems for evaluating movement of groups toward desirable goals. Bernstein (1952), for example, was one of the first to describe a set of criteria and a scale for measuring group progress. He used criteria such as attendance, ability to plan, cohesiveness, need for the leader, handling of intra-group conflict and the like. In this approach, a picture of development is achieved through observation of progress along these various dimensions over periods of time. Trecker (1955) follows a somewhat similar course when he states: "The usual signs of group development include such things as more prompt and constant attendance by members, decision on a definite meeting time and place, development of formal organization, and a willingness on the part of members to take responsibility for the work of the group. Criteria such as these provide useful guide lines for charting group movement and for delineating the significant dimensions and phenomena associated with it. There are important limits, however, to the use we make of these criteria in our attempts to understand group development.

Apart from the mechanical complexities associated with scale construction, there are three basic phenomena with which the criterion model by itself does not deal. The first of these is the general state of development; it has not been possible to "add up the scores" that a group achieves along the various dimensions on a chart such as Bernstein's and come up with a number representing the state of progress. Nor has there been a non-numerical method for combining the dimensions at a particular point, to characterize a general picture of development. Changes along any two dimensions may not only be unequal but in different directions at the same time. A group may be highly cohesive but in great conflict with authority. Another group may have high intra-group conflict and tension on the one hand, but high average attendance on the other.[3] The second related phenomenon is retrogression; a group may show a great deal of positive change along one or more dimensions and then, at a later date, slide backwards. A familiar case in point is the group which develops all the trappings of formal organization (e.g., officers, business meetings, dues, etc.) but several weeks later chucks the whole business and wants to be completely dependent on the group worker.

It is only within the context of a conceptual system dealing with the evolving process and problem-phases of interaction among members that the movement scale becomes a dynamic and flexible tool. In other words, attempts at measurement of movement or change can have most evaluative significance when they are related to a theory of development.

Theories of Group Development

Numerous theories and models having to do with general cycles and phases of group development have been proposed, mostly from the group therapy and human relations training fields. Social psychology, focusing on communication work and decision-making areas has contributed also. Studies in this vein on the part of social workers have been few but merit attention. In considering

---

[3] Bernstein has, since his original study, focused intensively on this conflict dimension. His present view is that the intensification of open conflict may, at times, be seen as an index of health rather than as a sign of pathology. See his "Conflict in Group Work", the next article in this book.

group movement in a global context, Trecker has described loosely an evolving six-stage model.[4] The framework which he presents is one which portrays groups in their progress from a "pre-group" aggregate of individuals up to a high point of optional cohesion, through a naturally and mutually agreed upon dissolution. Trecker cautions us that these six stages are not always fully apparent, that there is retrogression at times, and that leaders should not encourage groups to attempt projects or activities which are beyond their developmental level. Kindlesperger, without giving attention to specific indices of change, presents a more rigorously delineated outline in which he sees six stages of group development going from a first stage of approach or orientation to various stages of negotiation and group-role emergence and dominance.[5] His focus in general appears to be the satisfaction of personal needs through the assumption of various roles, and he stresses the importance of working through to a point where the group is capable of functioning well as a unit and producing a product. This formulation appears to be a very useful start; however, it would seem that for general social group work purposes an orientation which focuses more specifically on the ego needs of individuals within the group without demanding production of the group in relation to "The outside" would be more appropriate. Henry Maier and his associates are at present engaged in a project to test a set of hypotheses related to a phase of group development.[6] Four phases have been proposed. They are: (1) Locating commonness, (2) Creating exchange, (3) Developing mutual identification, and (4) Developing group identification. Maier sees the small group naturally starting at phase one and progressing through each succeeding phase in order. His investigation also involves identification of interactions that may be located at particular phases. Such a thorough and detailed study would appear to be potentially of great value for a distinctly social work-oriented theory of group development. Austin describes six steps that have been observed in the process of work with delinquent gangs.[7] Although he focuses more on

[4] Trecker. *Op. Cit.,* pp. 92–93.

[5] Kindlesperger. *Op. Cit.*

[6] Maier, Henry W. and Associates, Research, Group Development, 1961–1962. University of Washington, School of Social Work, Seattle.

[7] Austin, David. "Goals for Gang Workers", *Social Work,* Vol. 2, No. 4, October, 1957, pp. 43–50.

development from the standpoint of worker-group relationship (i.e., interaction, termination), implications for the development of a mature, socially responsible group system are evident. Helen Northen, also writing on group work delinquents, traces the development of the group and the helping process through several problem stages.[8] She does not label all of these phases specifically, but gives a clinically rich description of the various problems and tasks that members face, how they become increasingly able to face and master these problems, and how action of the worker facilitates the process. The flavor of her presentation closely resembles the model which we shall describe.

When we consider ideas about the nature of the group experience that have been advanced by practitioners in fields related to social group work, we find a wide variety of opinions. These usually reflect the particular writer's base in practice and the kind of use to which he wishes to put his group. It will be found from examining a number of these different formulations that the groups described by the writers generally tend to locate themselves along a continuum which ranges from highly cohesive task-oriented groups in which there is submission of individual needs and desires to the good of the group, to a completely loose-knit "compresence" of individuals, each meeting his own needs without particular concern as to what happens to other people in the group or whether the group ever really becomes a group. Slavson[9] and others[10] have drawn distinctions between social work and so-called "ordinary" groups on the one hand and psycho-therapeutic groups on the other which generally follow this continuum, and have emphasized the varying degrees of basic personality re-orientation and restructuring to be derived from these various types of groups.

Homans, in his analysis of small groups, does not identify problem stages as such, but has posed a recurring and reciprocal

---

[8] Northen, *Op. Cit.*

[9] Slavson, S. R. "Common Sources of Error and Confusion in Group Psychotherapy", *International Journal of Group Psychotherapy,* Vol. 3, No. 1, Jan. 1953, pp. 19–22.

[10] Grace, Priscilla B. "A Scheme for Differentiating Therapeutic Group Work from Group Psychotherapy". Unpublished Master's thesis, Boston University School of Social Work, 1960, and Scheidlinger, Saul. "The Concept of Social Group Work and of Group Psychotherapy", *Social Case Work,* Vol. 34, No. 7, July, 1953, pp. 292–297.

cycle, with activity, interaction and sentiment being the processual ingredients of formation.[11] Semrad and Arensenian have identified ". . . a sequence of phases of group activity that is seen along with the varied responses (of individual members) and is characteristic even where the responses vary widely".[12] They have dealt with groups of staff members and mental hospital patients, and feel that, regardless of membership, there is some unique quality about the group experience which necessitates a working through of a certain range of problems in inter-relationships. They have identified (1) a phase of orientation, (2) a phase of feeling out or testing, (3) a phase of resistance, and (4) a phase in which, having identified their own attitudes and roles within the group, members begin to borrow desirable traits from the central figure (therapist), and actively share feelings and support one another as they discuss their group relationships and problems. They identifiy clique formation, ambivalence about closeness and problems around cohesion. Semrad, in another article with Standish[13] identifies four stages: The first phase which is a testing-out situation in which hostility toward the hospital (i.e., a state mental institution) creates group unity, the second, in which anxiety-laden psychotic fantasies are freely expressed, the third, during which feelings toward one another are shared and introspective thinking is done, and the fourth, a closing phase, in which members begin to focus on the outside world and make plans for what they will do when they leave the institution. Initial hostile verbal activity toward the hospital is seen as a result of anxiety over being in the group and resistance to joining this close emotional situation. Semrad and Standish point out that there are many references in speech to violence and destruction during these early phases.

Mann has identified quite similar stages of development.[14] He has developed some general theoretical notions about the

[11] Homans, George C. *The Human Group.* New York: Harcourt, Brace and Company, 1950.

[12] Semrad, Elvin V. and John Arsenian. "The Use of Group Processes in Teaching Group Dynamics", *American Journal of Psychiatry,* Vol. 108, Nov. 1951, p. 360.

[13] Standish, Christopher T. and Elvin V. Semrad. "Group Psychotherapy with Psychotics", *Journal of Psychiatric Social Work,* Vol. 20, No. 4, June, 1951, pp. 143–150.

[14] Mann, James. "Analytically Oriented Study of Groups", *Journal of Psychiatric Social Work,* Vol. 20, No. 4, June, 1951, pp. 137–43.

problems that individuals must work through in making use of a group and feels that: ". . . each group member tends to react with hostility to the anxiety induced by the special setting of group therapy, that is, a setting in which each is forced to be close to others. Without the working through of such defensive hostility a firm barrier continues to exist, a barrier which often is missed by the therapist because the group looks like it is functioning well, whereas in reality, each member has maintained very successfully a protective shell which serves to perpetuate his isolation and to prevent real involvement in the group".[15]

Bennis, writing from the point of view of the human relations trainer with an interest in the therapeutic overtones of the "T" group and in breaking down barriers to communication, has worked out a two-phase dependence-interdependence developmental model[16]: He sees a progression through six sub-phases where the members struggle with orientation, power and organization problems and come to an end point of more intimate interdependence. Thelen and Dickerman come to pretty much similar conclusions,[17] although their phase descriptions do not have the vivid quality of Bennis' "fight-flight" characterization. Schutz proposes an inclusion-control-effection progression,[18] which, like Bennis, shows more closely to the psychiatrically based models. In addition, he makes use of a cyclical theory to account for the recurrence of certain problem situations which is somewhat reminiscent of Homans's model.[19]

[15] Mann, James. "Some Theoretic Concepts of the Group Process", *The International Journal of Group Psychotherapy,* Vol. 5, No. 3, July, 1955, p. 236.

[16] Bennis, Warren G. and H. A. Shepard. "A Theory of Group Dynamics", *Human Relations,* Vol. 9, No. 4, 1956, pp. 415–457.

[17] Thelen, Herbert and Watson Dickerman. "Stereotypes and the Growth of Groups", *Educational Leadership,* Vol. 6, No. 5, Feb. 1949, pp. 309–316.

[18] Schutz, William C. "The Interpersonal Underworld", *Harvard Business Review,* Vol. 36, No. 4, July–August, 1958, pp. 123–135.

[19] This idea of "going around again" (Schutz uses the analogy of tightening bolts on an auto wheel) seems also to follow the line of thought expressed by Mary Follett who spoke of increasingly sophisticated resolution of life problems (e.g., conflict) as they are encountered and re-encountered. Follet, Mary P. *Creative Experience,* New York: Longmans, Green and Co., 1942, Ch. 3.

The writings cited above provide important clues to some of the significant dimensions in group development that must be considered.* Problems such as anxiety about interdependence among group members are common themes in all of them. The necessity for step-by-step progression through the various phases seems to be accepted by the model builders. In this regard, their models are, in general, similar to that which we propose, although they do not deal specifically with (1) the problem of ego support and maintenance of ego-defensive patterns in the face of the impact of the group, or (2) frames of reference for perception and behavior that appear during the course of group development.

The Model

We are now ready to describe a model consisting of *five stages of development* which the authors believe appear quite commonly in social work groups. Three of the assumptions upon which the model is based are: (1) that *closeness* is a central theme in the process and development of these groups, (2) that one can identify *frames of reference* that are employed by members for perception and behavior in the groups, and (3) that these frames of reference *change* as the character of the group experience changes. The model should provide a useful conceptual outline for the process and structure of a typical social work group. It is presented as a tool for practice to be used in conjunction with knowledge of individual and group psychology and management and programming techniques, and in the service of general work values and goals.

A. *Applicability*

Since the construction of our model was based primarily upon observations of formed club groups, whose members had not been closely associated prior to formation, its applicability may be limited to groups of this general type. A question may be posed as to whether this model would apply to other kinds of groups such as already-existing friendship groups that come into agencies in search of leadership, or to committee and other task groups. It is obvious, for instance, that if members have been friends prior

---

*We have discussed only a representative sample of many writings that have been done, especially in the group dynamics and human relations training fields.

to association with the social worker, there is a strong possibility, especially in the initial phases of coming together, that the form and quality of relationships will be affected. There is, however, an equally strong possibility that many of the problems with which these other groups have to deal are similar to those faced by the groups upon which the study is based. It remains for practitioners who are working with various types of groups to test the model to see where it does or does not apply. It may be that the model cannot embrace every kind of group but will serve as a helpful point of reference, an "ideal type", and as such provide a base for developing other models. The problem of the applicability of the model in relation to the varying goals and multitude of functions performed by group service agencies is also important. Here, again, practical testing must be undertaken and modifications made in terms of the orientations of particular agencies. It should be noted that the groups we used in our study represent both sexes, ages from 9 to 16, various levels of personality integration and social sophistication and different social classes. These variables, do not, we believe, seriously affect the applicability of the model, although the way in which members of one particular age or social class will deal with a developmental task may be different from the manner in which members of another age and class will handle it.

B. *The Problem of Self-fulfilling Prophecy*

The next question which must be faced is whether the model is descriptive or a normative one. Will the stages which are to be described always occur in a small group; or are the stages in effect created by the manipulation of the social worker? Will he make his own prediction come true? The answer appears to lie in the fact that although there is no one "natural" path of development that a small group must irresistibly take over a period of time, there does seem to be a definable *range* of courses that the group may follow; a range which may vary from extreme formality to extreme intimacy, or from high to low conformity, or from individually-oriented activity to close team work, to cite a few continua. The model is descriptive in that it attempts to show one type of "natural" development that may occur. At the same time, the range within which the worker permits or encourages the group to function, will be determined to a certain extent by the level or type of help he wishes to give the group. Thus, our model is *normative* in the sense that the social worker, as a group leader, operates at one particular level, and is interested primarily in providing opportunities for the enhancement of the ego functioning of individual members. He will encourage and respond to intimacy, interdependence and group cohesion in a way which is compatible with general social work aims regarding the maintenance and strengthening of those defenses and transactional skills which promote creative social adjustment.[20] In the sense that problems such as intimacy, defense against exploitation, cooperation, power struggles, etc., seem to be common to most small groups, the model should be useful in increasing our understanding of the dynamics of a number of groups, although it might be most specifically applicable to only a few.

C. *Method*

The method that was employed to form some preliminary ideas about the stages of development was mainly a clinical one. In the course of staff seminars or practice, we noted that behaviors exhibited by different groups seemed to reflect similar interpersonal issues and that these issues changed as time went on. The concepts concerning stages of group development which we began to construct to account over a three-year period for this were recountered in practice. This process has been done on an informal basis and findings drawn from records and practice observations have been largely subject to clinical interpretation. Validation of the ideas presented in the model will have to be done in clinical practice settings until such time as experimental settings and methods are adequate and available to do the job.

D. *Central Theme*

The central theme running through all of these stages, as we have indicated, is that of closeness. From the moment that a number of individuals consent to be together in one spot, through the period during which they make their first tentative efforts to acquaint themselves with and find satisfaction in one another, on through the time when they share the intense feelings they have

---

[20] For an elaboration on the use of "support" as a major tool in social group work and its relationship to *generic social* work ego-oriented methods, see Frey, Louise A. "Support and the Group: A Generic Treatment Form", *Social Work*, Vol. 7, No. 41, October, 1962, pp. 35–40.

toward one another, until the dissolution of their common bond, they must struggle with how near they will come to one another emotionally. Manifestations of this phenomenon are constantly made evident in group life. We observe it in connection with physical proximity (who sits next to whom), in a member's selection of activities (solitary crafts compared to tackle football), in the extent of his willingness to cooperate and be governed by the group (a club constitution, rules on spending money for refreshments), and in direct verbal expression ("Anne is a louse for quitting the club — I liked her better than anyone.") Even the changes which occur in the frames of reference that members typically employ to orient themselves and to give meaning to the group experience, as it continues, appear to reflect an increase in intimacy and closeness. The group is seen at first in the light of other clubs, classes or groups, then as a family-style gathering and later as an experience in and of itself, with a unique and autonomous identity. With termination of the group the change reverses, and as separation proceeds the group becomes a frame of reference for new social experiences.

It can be argued that as central themes, dimensions such as cooperation or communication or group identity are at least as significant as closeness. We are emphasizing closeness because, in addition to the fact that it has qualities common to these other dimensions, it seems to convey best the sense that the group experience involves social beings and human emotions.

E. *Stages of Development*

The five stages of growth — problem levels through which members and group as a whole pass in the course of their development are: (1) pre-affiliation, (2) power and control, (3) intimacy, (4) differentiation, and (5) separation.

Stage 1. Pre-affiliation — approach and avoidance

The initial period of group association is one in which the members are becoming familiar with one another and the situation, and have not yet formed close ties. Relationships are usually non-intimate and a good deal of use may be made of rather stereotypic activity as a means of getting acquainted and at the same time retaining some distance and protection. The group and the worker tend to be seen as reflections of other groups and leaders with which the individual has had contact in his social experience (as distinguished from family experience). Members' ambivalence toward involvement is reflected in their vacillating response to program activities and events. An on-again-off-again attitude toward such things as parallel versus interactive play, accepting versus not accepting, and responsibility verus avoidance in cleanup and planning are quite common. The basic struggle in this ambivalent, pre-affiliative phase, when viewed in the light of the closeness dimension, is one of approach and avoidance. Whether the group members elect officers and plan a month in advance at the first meeting or lurk outside the club room furtively peeking in the door, they are probably experiencing some kind of anxiety about becoming involved and are attempting to find ways within their framework of social experience to accomplish this process of exploration and affiliation.

The following case material describes in detail some of the typical kinds of behavior manifested in the initial phases of group life. In line with our thesis of *closeness* as a central theme and *approach-avoidance* as the major early struggle in relation to it, this material suggests the following propositions: (1) that during initial meetings the same behavior may enable members simultaneously to explore the situation and avoid close involvement in it, (2) that divergent behavior may have common purposes (exploration and protection), (3) that the way in which the approach-avoidance situation is managed gives important clues to individual ego defenses, and (4) that cautious "arms length" exploration at this pre-affiliative stage is essentially a healthy process and may be used as a model against which diagnostic impressions may be checked.

The Hotshots

The Hotshots, a group of six ten year old boys from immigrant lower-class families, representing a normal range of strength and problems, held their first meeting in a large basement room of a settlement house. All of the boys, with the exception of Tony, an impulsive, severely disturbed, foreign-born youngster, were members of the settlement and participated regularly in its varied program of activities. Previous to this group they had had only casual contacts with one another. The first thing that the boys did was to explore the room, going into cupboards and the like. Tony, arriving with a bag of bread and fried fish clutched in one hand, found a bicycle and wheeled this around the periphery of the room avoiding the others. The other five members asked the worker "what do we have to do in this club?", as if the worker had a prescribed program they had to follow. They were extremely enthusiastic in responding to suggestions that the worker made about trips and activities. One member wanted immediately to elect officers. After they played an active game, the boys began to turn out the lights and wrestle with each other and again began to look into cupboards and explore. In the handling of soda and cookies, furnished by the worker, they shared politely and only one took an extra cookie, stealing this from Tony. After they had the food, there was hiding again. During the course of this meeting, perhaps fearful that some of the members didn't know him, Tony asked one youngster, "Hey, do you know me?"

For the second meeting, the Hotshots had planned to make some French fries in a different room which had a kitchen and was in a building a short walk from the settlement house. Tony was late meeting with the boys at the settlement house, and the others at first did not want to wait for him. When he did arrive, he mumbled that he hadn't been sure that there was going to be a meeting (the worker had sent postal cards to all the boys). The boys asked a lot of questions about trips they could go on and activities they could do. They explored a little at the new room but were able to start quickly on the activity, peeling and cooking potatoes. Tony, who had to go to the bathroom immediately, avoided the others by playing a record player a great deal. He did this off and on for the better part of the afternoon. One member had a real fight with him and then withdrew guiltily. This was a boy who had not come to the first meeting. The boys didn't stick with the activity very long but were able to play organized games that the worker set up. When the food was laid out in front of them they stole potatoes from one another in contrast to their more conventional handling of food the week before.

The Smoothies

The Smoothies were a group of five lower-class ten-year old boys, all described as being well-behaved and productive in school.

Two of the boys were somewhat socially isolated, one of them being rather effeminate. The boys knew that the group had been formed to help Gary, the effeminate youngster, to make new friends. At the first meeting, the boys tumbled over one another verbally in talking to one another and to the worker about where each of them lived, movies, and t.v. Their behavior was conventional although hyperactive. They were awed by the settlement house where they were going to meet, none having been members previously. They were well behaved here and extremely polite to one another and to the worker. One of the members said he was awfully hungry and immediately began to eat with relish when the worker provided the food. The boys talked incessantly about the scenery, about t.v. and the movies. One of the members was relieved when the worker told him where the bathroom was and he went in. The others immediately trooped in after him. Later they were more relaxed. They hid on the worker. They enjoyed the active game that they played. The worker noted later that their laughter seemed forced. They discussed plans for the future avidly and latched on to the worker's suggestions for games easily. At one point, one of the members put his arms around Gary and Gary hugged back. They all hugged each other and came close as they decided on a song to sing. They wrestled and hid again and giggled a good deal. The worker noted that when he let one youngster off at home he ran out of the car and into his house without saying a word. One of the boys said that there would be no school the next week and asked if something special could be held. One of the other members told a new member excitedly about the "club house" and the others joined in.

The next week: The whole group was extremely helpful in passing out refreshments on the outing. While they were eating one of the boys brought up the subject of illness and talked about his uncle's operation; another youngster spoke of his mother's illness. One of the boys talked about Easter presents and then another who had led off the discussion of illness talked about rockets and rocket ships and heaven, and how "you can't get there even with rocket ships". There was some dispute over whether St. Mary was up in Heaven too, which was raised by one of the youngsters, but no real argument. The new member told the worker, after about an hour, "I love this club!" The boys talked about Martians and described them in terms of a bizarre and horrible war between Mars and Earth and the like and rockets. One of the boys said he liked to design rockets and when the worker asked the boys what they'd like to be they all answered this quite easily. Gary started to hang back at this point and to exhibit some dreaminess. Again the conventional behavior came out quite clearly as while the boys were going through the park near the zoo one of them asked the worker if they could run and the worker said, "Certainly". There was no problem of control here, although they giggled some when they watched the animals excreting.

The Belles

The first two meetings of the Belles, an institutional adolescent girls' group, revealed certain patterns clearly. This group was made up of ten members. The girls were in the institution because of delinquent or pre-delinquent behavior. The group already was a group in a sense, and coming to the club had some compulsory aspects. During the first meeting there was polite acceptance of the worker when any staff members were present. As soon as the staff had left the room, the girls began to talk against the staff in the worker's presence. They talked "around" the leader, using pig latin for example. The talked with hostility against their teachers as the worker listened to their complaints about the staff. At one point one of the girls said, "ssh-ssh, she's beginning to talk". The members turned to the worker asking "What are we going to do?" When the worker asked what they would like to do they responded with many organizational suggestions. Testing of the worker occurred in the form of repeated use of pig latin and Italian obscenities, followed by asking her if she knew what these meant. The members responded extremely enthusiastically to any program suggestions which the worker made. They talked about doing all sorts of things outside the institution. Yet, when the choice was left up to them, they indicated that they wanted to do something closer to home. They asked for simple crafts. The first meeting ended on a high note. The members were all set on what to do for the next week and eagerly wanted it.

The next week, the Belle's responses were strikingly different from that of the preceding week. Some of the youngsters were watching t.v. when the worker came in. They acted in a covertly hostile way toward the leader, barely looking at her when she came in. They gathered slowly and asked lethargically, "What are we going to do this week?", even though they had planned the crafts the week before. Each member responded individually, some liking the crafts and some not. There was little, if any, cooperative effort in contrast to all the talk of the week before about "We'll do this". There was a good deal of asking for help from the worker. Conversation was more guarded than the week before. Some of the girls did not touch refreshments that the worker laid out. There was no mention of complaints against the staff at this meeting as there had been the week before.

The Tendency to Approach:

One of the first things that is evident in all of the above examples, is the desire that the members have for the group experience. They attempt to explore its possibilities and make beginning efforts to organize themselves to make some use of it. For the most part, they pounce eagerly on the refreshments and the activities presented by the worker. They asked excitedly about future program possibilities. Many of them, putting their best foot forward, exhibit polite, conventional behavior. The Hotshots set up a feeding session (French fries) for their second meeting. Past club experiences are discussed and many personal references are made. Plans are made for future meetings, ranging from agreements such as offering to bring a potato, to suggestions that officers be elected to carry on the business of group life. In short, there is considerable evidence that the children from the start want to become involved in and make use of what the group and the worker have to offer.

The Tendency to Avoid:

In contrast to the moves toward involvement in all three groups are the tendencies toward avoidance and maintaining distance. Tony operates literally on the periphery of the Hotshots during the first meeting, then arrives late for the second meeting. The boys in the well-behaved Smoothies group are pleasantly excited, but they also have to escape from the worker and the room when at one point, en masse, they quickly follow one of the members who asks to go to the bathroom. Although the Belles plan the program at their first meeting with apparent eagerness, when the worker appears for the second meeting they ask her lethargically, "What are we going to do?" Fearful of being obligated to a giver,

34

or of being deprived, Tony comes to the first meeting with food of his own. Wariness in regard to the same problem of involvement and dependency is exhibited by some of the Belles as they hesitate to accept food or craft materials. The Smoothies talk of Martians and illness and destruction. Such topics appear with remarkable regularity in early group meetings, and probably reflect fear of the strangeness of the new experiences and concern over being attacked by the worker or other members.

Initially, then we see activity from "proper" deferential behavior, accompanied by attempts to organize and plan on an apparently sophisticated level, to impulsive examination of the environment and even destructive attack upon it. In respect to degree of involvement, we observe behavior ranging from almost frantic exploration and attempts at incorporation of the club room and its equipment, to a reluctance to use any of the available material or even, on occasion, to enter the room.

In exploring the motivations that underlie this wide range of behaviors, it is important first to consider the individual member's perception of the situation as he enters the group. The questions which consciously or unconsciously are likely to concern him are: What is the leader going to be like: Is he like the school teacher, the cop, my parents, the last leader I had? Is he strict? Will he give things to me? What do I have to do to make him like me? What are the other members like: bigger, stronger, weaker, smarter, "dumber" than me? Whom will the leader like best? Can they do things better than I can? Do I have to share things? Will we have fun together? Is this all really worth taking a chance on?

As we suggested, these questions reflect two major, divergent tendencies operating in the member's mind at this point: the tendency to approach and to involve himself in the situation because of the gratifications which it promises, and the tendency to avoid the situation because of the demands, the frustrations and even the pain which he may anticipate. The resolution of this dilemma appears to lie in the member's use of a set of behaviors which satisfies both of these tendencies simultaneously, i.e., which facilitates exploration of the situation and at the same time permits some distance and protection from close improvement. For example, when the Hotshots turn out the lights and hidden from the worker, act out, they are performing at least two functions. Most obviously, they are hiding or avoiding. At the same time, they are exploring and approaching by virtue of defining the limits of permissible behavior, and, testing one another's nerve and power in this new situation. Similarly the Belles as they express hostility toward teachers and other adults, and Tony as he cruises around the room, are scouting issues and relationships at the same time that they are skirting them.

All the children described here seemed to be faced with similar approach-avoidance alternatives. Suggested in this context is our second corollary: that behaviors which are ostensibly quite dissimilar may reflect similar needs and serve similar *skirting* and *scouting* functions. The girl who sits and watches t.v. turning her back in the craft session, the boy who rides his bike around the room, or the youngster who hovers around in the hallway outside, are obviously holding themselves back from involvement. In the same way, the child who runs about wildly, exploring, making noise, etc., though his impulse control is obviously poorer, may be guarding against psychic contact with his fellows. Less obviously, the boy who immediately suggests setting up formal club rules, collecting dues, planning program for several weeks in advance, or who very solicitously helps other members and the leader clean up, may also be protecting himself from too close association, at the same time that he is receiving gratification from the group experience through this formal behavior.

The Frame of Reference — Society:
We have examined some of the emotional pulls and coping devices associated with initial group contact. We now turn to the matter of how members perceive the group and the worker, since their perception influences greatly how they feel about making an affiliation, and, as we shall suggest, is in turn shaped by these feelings. Observation of member's behavior indicates that they begin the process of entry and adjustment by establishing a frame of reference whereby the new situation may be rendered understandable and predictable. Members draw upon those past experiences which appear similar to the present one, and in so doing find continuity, and meaning, as well as a basis for assessing the potentialities for gratification and for orienting their own conduct in the group. The social work group in this early stage typically resembles other types of "social groups" (e.g., the scout troop, the handicraft club, the Sunday school class, the athletic team, etc.) and provides, as most

36

members perceive it, an image that is familiar and relatively non-intimate. Thus, perception of the group is conditioned primarily at this point by social experiences outside the family. Consequently, we speak of the frame of reference used by members as "societal" rather than familial.*

The familiar, protective activity structure on the one hand, and the implication that the experience involves growth and change on the other, set the stage for a moderately paced process of affiliation. In this connection, we must emphasize that the societal frame of reference is involved not only because it is familiar, but also because of the *need* and *desire* to avoid closeness. That is to say, not only does the group worker *look* like a crafts instructor because he brings paints and paper to the first meeting; it is also not *safe* at this early point to see him in a more intimate light, even though members may basically desire and later seek a closer, more dependent relationship with him.

Selection of specific program activities and interactional patterns by members is influenced by the frame of reference they employ and the image they have of the group as well as by the approach – avoidance tensions present (e.g., in all of the three groups described safe, familiar activities were selected for second meetings). Other factors, of course, enter in also, such as materials and directions provided by the worker and physical setting – one can hide (avoid) in a basement room by turning out the lights, in a park, by running. Tony's clinging to fish and bread and the Belles' use of Italian swear words suggest that selection of behavior is determined also by particular social backgrounds and by individual personality structures as well. It is to this last named area that we wish to turn next.

Pre-Affiliation and Normality:

We have considered some general problems that arise out of initial group association. We must now examine the matter of the impact of this association on individuals with varying degrees of personality integration and social maturity, and ask whether the approach-avoidance model is equally applicable to healthy and

---

*We are aware that family experiences have conditioned perceptions of society and that family is in a sense part of society. However, the influence of the family during this stage seems to be at the most a derivative, indirect one and verbal and behavioral references are mainly to extra-familial experience.

disturbed individuals. Two points seem to be evident from the examination of our record material: (1) "Good" or organized behavior does not seem to be necessarily an evidence of maturity (although healthier members do seem generally more able to involve themselves, at least at the very outset, in quite a proper and controlled manner). (2) Initial ability to maintain control over perceptions and behavior (in regard to such things as trying to engulf immediately the leader or other group members, striking out at people or physical surroundings or committing one's self or exposing one's self to an unusual degree) seems to reflect some degree of ego-organization and impulse control, even though, in some cases, this ability would be seen as temporary and might break down considerably during later meetings. We have already mentioned some of the anxieties which group members may feel at the beginning of the group experience. In the social work group, the anxiety may have a more pervasive quality due to the lack of an assigned task on the one hand, and the expectation of change on the other. Keeping in mind our hypothesis that there is an attempt by the ego to maintain some sort of internal control during initial group meetings, it seems accurate to think of many of the adaptive attempts illustrated in the record material we have presented as being essentially healthy. This is to say, the ego in order to preserve its integrity and protect itself from injury in this new (and potentially harmful) situation, needs to maintain a certain amount of distance and control over the actions of the individual and over the external situation as well. This kind of cautious, arm's length exploration thus enables the person to obtain the gratifications that he perceives to be present, but with a minimum of risk. Perhaps an example of an ego which is unable to protect itself will serve to illuminate this point. The following were the reactions of Tom, a pre-delinquent boy in early adolescence, at the first meeting of his group.

Tom's first statement when he arrived at the meeting was that he had forgotten about the meeting until another youngster reminded him. The activity for the meeting was fishing and Tom fished away from the other youngsters. He initiated conversation with the worker a good deal. He disparaged his own fishing skills in comparison with his brother's, but said he is a good hunter. He asked the worker whether they could smoke and the worker replied that they could if they had permission from their parents. One of the other members made suggestions about trips and forming a baseball team for the club. Tom questioned whether they could fit nine into the car. When the other boys began fighting in the back of the car on the ride back from fishing, Tom kept telling them to calm down. He turned to them and said that the worker would not take them anymore if they kept up this kind of behavior. He got into an argument with the other youngsters about whether he talked too much about his material possessions.

Prior to the second meeting of the club, Tom invited the worker into his house to see his new boots. There were long stretches of silence and Tom seemed very depressed at the start of this second meeting. He talked about his father who is not living in the same house as he, and said that his father was going to bring him fireworks. He also asked if the worker could come up the next time for a whole day. The group became lost doing some hill climbing but took the frustration quite well. Tom, at one point, said he was feeling very tired and said, "I want to die". When the worker offered the boys ice cream cones, Tom said, "I don't care". When the worker kidded him about this a bit, Tom said, with a broad smile that he really wanted some. He began fooling around with the first aid kit and asked if the mercurochrome was poisonous.

The essential difference between Tom's reaction and those illustrated by the other records are that: (1) Tom seems to need very much to ally himself with the worker, to get very close to him and to separate himself very actively from the other youngsters. (2) He almost immediately brings in personal material in a meaningful way. He compares himself to his brother. This may possibly be a reflection of his anxiety in relation to the other boys. It does not appear from examination of many group records, however, that children typically bring in this kind of family reflection, so early in the group experience, especially in a way that is obviously so emotionally charged. Tom also brings up during the second meeting the fact of his father not living with him and immediately after this, talks about the father bringing to him fireworks. (3) Related to this personal material and to Tom's need to separate himself from the other boys is his insistence to them that they behave themselves. It would seem on this point that Tim is quite close to telling the leader already about how afraid he is of losing control and how closely this is related to some of his family problems. (4) He unmasks his depression quite directly to the worker by stating with a good deal of affect that he wants to die. (5) In connection with this, he expresses his ambivalence about being fed by the worker but then indicates immediately how much he wants the ice cream. After this, he begins to talk about the possibility of being poisoned by the medicine that is present in the worker's car.

Some of Tom's ways of handling his anxiety in those first two meetings are typical of the defenses employed by some of the more normal children and some of the disturbed children mentioned previously. However, the essential difference appears to be that Tom is really so much in need of this immediate relationship with the adult that he is unable to be cautious and must rush in immediately to involve himself with the worker. In this connection, he makes direct reference to siblings and parents and seems to be almost consciously connecting the group with his family. At the same time, he is unable to cover up his ambivalent feelings in regard to this dependency which he desires so much; i.e., he discusses poison almost immediately after accepting an ice cream cone from the worker.

He also indicates his general emotional tone directly by saying, "I want to die". It seems that Tom at this early point in the group experience is unable to muster enough ego defenses to behave either appropriately in the social sense, or to hold himself aloof from a relationship with the adult. It is significant that the observations made in these initial meetings regarding the difficulty Tom was having with his defenses were borne out later by his behavior in the group and by further information regarding his problems around the community and at home.

There are three other types of situations that have been observed in which clients make immediate reference to family and personal material in a manner ostensibly similar to Tom's. These may be distinguished from Tom's reaction, however, in that they do not arise primarily from a disordered personality structure.

The first example involves the person who has led a culturally typical, protected existence. Jean was an emotionally stable girl of fifteen from an immigrant family who had been very closely bound to home. Although she was an adolescent and would be commonly expected to relate principally to her peers. Jean immediately made a very close relationship with the worker and began to treat her almost immediately as a mother substitute. She had had such limited social experience that she had no real frame of reference in American society in general against which to compare the group.

The second situation is that of the child who has built up a set of standards and expectations revolving around his sickness. One such child was Althea, a schizophrenic adolescent who had spent some time in a state hospital and was subsequently in therapy for several years. At the first meeting of her club, Althea began almost immediately to make references to her psychiatrist as a means of entering into conversation. In this case a dual interpretation may be made of her behavior. The obvious fact is that Althea had a severely impaired ego and was probably unable to operate on any but an extremely dependent level. Another fact, however, is that some of the meaningful people in Althea's existence had been psychiatrists. So, she, in a very real sense, was using her own social experience, atypical though it may have been, as a frame of reference in approaching her peers and her group worker, and in presenting herself to them.

The third category is that of very young children. They have typically had relatively little social contact outside the family, and their egos are still in the process of being formed. They tend, in general, to become more quickly involved and probably use the family immediately as a frame of reference for the group experience.

Implications for Diagnosis:

If the approach-avoidance problem is seen as a normal condition of early group life, the way in which members manage it may yield valuable material for the diagnosis of ego functioning. Temporary assumption of a relatively non-intimate relationship appears to be essentially appropriate. "Happy medium" criteria may be visualized both in terms of the quality and the duration of this relationship. The child who must invest all his energy in a wild avoidance of his peers and worker, or the one like Tom, who is unable to maintain distance from the adult, are examples of qualitative variations within the distance dimension. In regard to the duration question, Tom, who moves close too quickly, might be contrasted with the child who must cling for many months to formalized group structure as a protection against exposure or engulfment. These tests of the quality of involvement and the length of time required to clear the approach-avoidance hurdle may be useful in individual diagnosis when employed along with other knowledge that the worker possesses, such as, family background and functioning in other social settings. Considerable information bearing on matters such as the definitions of ego boundaries, rigidity of defensive patterns, nature of previous social experience, level of impulse control, and ability to form appropriate object relations may be gleaned from observations of behavior during this pre-affiliative stage.*

Worker Focus:

The worker, in order to help members to explore and to work on their involvement at a safe pace, should allow distance, furnish information regarding the operation of the group, encourage exploration of the physical setting and gently invite trust. His offering of snacks to a wary adolescent group, for example, may be done simply by putting food on the table and indicating its availability, thus not demanding that the food (and consequent dependency) be accepted or that members all sit around the table to eat it. He should be prepared to provide a good deal of program structure and if necessary introduce activities that minimize frustration and competitive interaction and ensure quick initial satisfaction and success. In this way, the individual member can secure gratifications without too much self exposure. He should probably not challenge the group's capacity for initiation of activity or for cooperative planning at this point. Although he stands ready to support group efforts in this direction, he should make it plain that his approval and affection are not conditioned by the presence or absence of such efficiency or investment.

Stage 2. Power and control

Once the basic problem has been solved as to whether the group experience is potentially safe and rewarding, and worth a preliminary emotional investment, members begin to lock horns with the power and control issues of group life. The problems of status, ranking, communication, choice making

---

*Although we shall not focus, in discussion of stages two through five, on individual diagnosis in relation to selection of coping behaviors, duration of stage, etc., the relevance of these indices should be kept in mind. They represent a challenging area for further study.

and "influence" come to the fore. There is a testing of the group worker and other members, and an attempt to define and formalize relationships and to create a status hierarchy. Physical strength, aggressiveness, mental agility and skill in whatever endeavors the group considers to be of high value must be discovered. Cliques form and alliances are made, at times for the purposes of mutual protection. These may vary in size from two against the group to the total group against one. This latter situation, sometimes arises out of the need of the group to protect itself from a very powerful and aggressive member, or from the psychic danger posed by a deviant or handicapped member. It is at this time that scapegoating first appears and, with it, an attempt to exclude individuals from membership.

The relationship which appears to be most significant in connection with the power-control issue and which has the greatest effect on the nature and intensity of intra-group control dynamics is that between the worker and group. The worker has the ability to give or withhold in material or emotional terms and this may include food, handicraft materials, the use of sporting equipment, a meeting room or an automobile, extra time for meetings, or personal attention for individuals. His role as therapist, teacher, parent, agency, community or social class representative, however the group perceives him, gives him a potential for influencing the affairs of the members that is at the same time comforting and overwhelming. A rather striking example of the impact of this potential is the amount of energy an anti-social gang will sometimes invest in keeping the group worker from being admitted into their system and from "taking over". Less dramatic, but often unsettling to the unwary worker, are the familiar examples of secretive whispering in the corner on the part of latency age girls, or the sudden willingness of a previously docile group of Golden Agers to accept the worker's program suggestions.

The Frame of Reference — Transition:
   It appears that the power and control stage represents a crucial period of transition. It is at the point that traditional value systems and familiar frames of reference do not prove adequate or useful as guides for evaluating the group situation. Whereas, during the initial meetings, members tended to view the experience as being

similar to other community groups they had known, during the stage two the character of the social work group assumes a unique and somewhat less definable quality. Therefore, the frame of reference for the power and control stage is, in a sense, a traditional one, and reflects the ambiguity and turmoil of change from a non-intimate to an intimate system of relationships.

Three basic issues are suggested by observation of power-struggle phenomena. The manner in which they are resolved will determine how successfully the struggle has been managed and whether the group will be able to face working through its next developmental tasks.

The first of these issues is that of *rebellion and autonomy.* Underlying this issue are questions such as the following: Can the worker permit the group to resist his authority within appropriate limits, so that they come to know that as individuals and collectively they have a degree of control over their own affairs and operation? Are the members assured that the worker, having agreed to their right to autonomy, also will agree to exercise restraint in the use of his power and will at the same time remain available for support and help?

The second issue, directly related to the first, is the *permission and the normative crisis.* We have implied that it is vital that the worker be non-punitive in the face of affronts to his authority, a necessary prerequisite to helping the members feel more secure in expressing themselves freely and in permitting autonomy in their relations with one another. It does not guarantee, however, that members will not initially, at least, become upset or frightened by this freedom, or that they will not continue repressive or scape-goating measures toward one another or attacks on their environ-ment. Witness the group of young adolescent boys who, after "desecrating" the club room walls with modelling clay, proceed to set up the "hot-oven" for the one member who uses dirty language in the worker's presence. Even though the worker indicates his acceptance of both hostile actions, they plead with the worker to "kick the pig out of the club". This is an example of the normative shock that is occasioned by the unfamiliar standards in regard to reward and punishment that the social worker presents. Where the worker gives tacit acceptance to the expression of anti-social feelings, familiar restraints are broken down. At the same time, the protection and expiatory comfort afforded by punishment are absent. The

44

two conditions together make for an anxiety-filled emotional vacuum, and group members compensate for this vacuum (and at the same time manage their own guilt and hostility) by trying to re-establish the traditional equilibrium. Some members, faced with these conditions, take flight, and record analysis and reports by workers suggest that the danger of dropouts at this point in the group's experience is relatively high.[21]

The third issue is one of *Protection and support.* The worker assures each member of a reasonable degree of safety from physical and psychic attack from the other members, as well as the control of his own attacks on the worker, other members or the physical environment. The worker's use of direct protective controls to the extent that they are necessary for continuance of group life also forestalls the development of a group structure based on a pecking order philosophy. This protection, along with the structure and support that are afforded by the activity program, indicates that individual expression rather than coercive conformity will be encouraged. At the same time, the tone is set for preservation of individual controls and ego-defenses. Program focus should be on activity that provides opportunities for mastery. Bowling, for example, a game that may provide for safety channeled release of aggression, opportunities for physical mastery of one's own body and inanimate objects, and competition on a somewhat pre-social basis, often is a welcomed activity at this time.*

Worker Focus:

In encouraging a balance that avoids repressive conformity on the one hand, and inhibits full-blown catharsis and regression on the

[21] Although the problem of dropouts in connection with normative shock is not specifically identified in group work literature, references have been made to this by writers in the clinical disciplines. Edith Varon, for example, feels that transition from "initial" to "middle" phases in adult therapy groups poses the threat of exposure and that more dropouts occur during this time than at any other. Varon, Edith. "Group Psychotherapy Transition from the Initial to the Middle Phase". Paper presented at Second Annual Institute of the Northeastern Society for Group Psychotherapy, Boston, April 25, 1958.

*This is not to say that program content *per se* completely determines the nature of interaction. Bowling may be used at a later date, for instance, as a way of playing out intense personal jealousies among members, or even later, in an inter-group tournament as an expression of group solidarity.

other, the social worker attempts to influence which course of development out of the range of possible natural courses the group will follow. He indicates the level of consciousness with which he is prepared to deal and the degree of mutual self-revelation among group members he will encourage. It is through the *clarification* with the group of the existence and nature of this power-control issue and its successful resolution that the group members become able to trust their vulnerable intimate selves to one another and to the worker.

As the worker clarifies issues in terms of their meaning in the here and now of the group, there is an opportunity for members to make a connection between a particular struggle in the group and similar struggles in their everyday lives. A familiar example of this is the case of the adolescent boys who suddenly demand the right to start smoking around the agency when they know perfectly well that smoking is not allowed. The worker takes a firm position on the necessity for observance of the rule within the agency and, as they react to this, considers with the boys, smoking and other "growing up" conflicts that arise between teenagers and adults. At the same time, he asks them to consider "What's going on right now between us," and focuses on their desire to pit their authority against his, indicating this is one of the natural things that happens between club members and club leaders. Clarification in this case, then, may deal not only with the member-worker power struggle within the group, but also with the desire of these youngsters as *adolescents* to begin to have natural control over their own affairs and to enter into the adult world. In considering the related questions of adolescent growth and group development, the boys can be helped to find ways of attaining a measure of autonomy in the conduct of their group affairs, without having to engage in continued and fruitless testing with the agency and the group worker over the matter. Implicit in this process, of course, is the significance of a crisis in group development as it reflects individual social and psychic development.[22]

---

[22] Eric Erikson's (1950) formation of the "eight stages of man" gives some excellent material for comparison of similarities between individual personality growth and group development (as outlined in this study). The value of this comparison lies not as much in trying to discover analogies between individual and group development, but in discovering how individual growth problems may be brought into the group and how group experience in turn may symbolize and facilitate the working through of these problems.

In all the above discussion, we see that the notion of contract is strongly evident. As they assure themselves of the worker's willingness and ability to maintain a safe balance in the power and control sphere and to allow autonomy and self-direction, the members make a firmer contract for service and for continuation of the group relationship on a new level of involvement.

Stage 3. Intimacy

The third stage of development is characterized by intensification of personal involvement, more willingness to bring into the open feelings regarding club members and worker and striving for satisfaction of dependency needs. Sibling-like rivalry tends to appear as well as overt comparisons of the group to family life. There is a growing ability to plan and carry out group projects, although this proficiency as interpersonal conflicts arise. There is a growing awareness and mutual recognition of the significance of the group experience in terms of personality growth and change.

As workers have looked at the control problems with which their groups have wrestled, they have noted, especially in retrospect, how much the struggle has had to do with intimacy. In the shock reaction that is occasioned by the worker's permissiveness, in the turmoil around deviance and conformity, may be seen the group's attempt to defend against intimacy. At the same time and through the same action, the desire to know and to be known, to share emotions arising out of common experience, and to become immersed in group life are made evident. In this sense, the power and control stage might be labelled as pre-intimacy, and the separation of stages two and three is somewhat arbitrary. The justification for distingusihing between power-control and intimacy rests principally on the fact that the members do at some point develop a system of relationships oriented to a more deeply personal, family-like model. They have firmly decided to "affiliate", and to play out the loves and hates that an intimate relationship involves.

The experience of the "Valiants", a group of five adolescent boys having a variety of physical and emotional problems, on a weekend camping trip, illustrates one way in which intimacy appears and some typical precursory conditions out of which it arises. During the first year of the club, the boys had functioned together on a superficial basis in planning and carrying out group activities. Discussion of personal problems or interests had been directed principally to the worker and mutual identification among members was practically non-existent. Conflict was limited mainly to arguing about choice of activity and mild physical bullying on the part of Jack, the biggest boy. Attempts to settle disputes consisted mainly of appeals to the worker. Program focused on easy trips in the community. Later, individually oriented crafts, with the use of woodworking tools became a prominent feature and provided opportunities for mastery and tentative expression of hostile feelings. Sam, the most physically handicapped member, derived great satisfaction in these craft sessions, and as spring of the club year approached, began to defend his rights in program planning discussions with greater assurance. When a spring camping weekend was proposed and the worker played a passive role in the planning, the boys became very anxious and angry with him, but finally battled out arrangements for menu, division of labor on buying, cooking, and cleanup, and choice of activities at camp. The struggle reached a climax at camp when the worker, during a baseball game, pointed out for the first time that Sam and Peter were using their awkwardness and physical problems as excuses to avoid aggressive action in the game. This evoked an explosion of anger against the worker and subsequent freeing up of Sam and Peter's energies to the extent that they won the game. Jack accepted the defeat of his side and, for the first time, let up in his nervous jibes at Sam. At the same time, the boys became noticeably more concerned about the amount of work each was doing at meal time. A good deal of argument erupted as to who was doing the most work and resentment was voiced for the first time toward affable, passive George for being selfish and only interested in himself. Riding home, the boys talked about the weekend and the club year. They focused their anger on the worker for making them plan their own weekend, and then reflected with some surprise on how well they had done. As they talked about other big events of the year, Peter expressed his anger and his sense of loss because Arthur was quitting the club to go out for the high school track team. This opened up the idea of how close the boys

48

were becoming and George again was criticized, this time in a pleading tone, because he always had "his God-damned ear in that portable radio". It was at this time, with Sam taking the lead, that the boys revealed to one another what had never been openly stated that they all had been or were in individual psychotherapy!

This condensed review of the Valiant's experience illustrates the steps involved in approaching and entering stage three. Individual mastery on a more or less non-interactive basis (e.g., Sam's use of tools) was a precursor to dealing with power relationships on the ground level. It will be noted that with these youngsters there was always complete reliance on the worker for protection; this is contra-distinction to the anti-social adolescent group's stand-offish approach, referred to previously. The transitional power struggle was exemplified in the group's planning for the overnight and playing the baseball game. Of assistance in solidifying the transition was the boys' verbal clarification of the movement toward autonomy which they had desired and resisted at the same time. The concerns that were manifest throughout the rest of the weekend are indicators of the intimate system of relationships that the boys were now beginning to accept. It is significant in this connection that all did not become peaceful and harmonious after the ball park crisis. Rather, a new level of problems was focused on. It suddenly became important how much one gave to and invested in the club, (e.g., criticism of self-centered George for being lazy, and of Arthur for leaving the group). Jealousy was directly reflected in arguments of who "always ate the most" and who "always" sat next to the worker in the car".

The worker's activity during the period of crisis and growing intimacy following the baseball game had three principal foci. There were (1) support for dependency needs, (2) stimulation of emergent growth crises, and (3) clarification of the growth. First, he maintained an essentially reassuring and giving posture. Earlier he had withdrawn from the planning and forced the group to function independently. Now in the face of this new turmoil and opening-up process, he took action at several points to allow less group effort. For example, he took initiative himself in going into a store to buy milk, while a hot argument over sharing money for treats was going on in the car. He also, at that time, bought milk which was in excess of the amount that the boys had budgeted for. In taking this kind of action, he furnished support in the face of the disorganization and regression that were triggered by the emergence of the new set of problems. Secondly, at other points, he aided and abetted the emergence of inter-personal strife. After a stiff argument over sharing had erupted at lunch time on the last day of the trip, for instance, the worker stimulated the conflict by asking who was supposed to dish up the ice cream. George had been assigned the job by the group, and when he resisted a new wave of heated discussion ensued. Finally, he helped the group to evaluate the weekend as it related to the club year, and, in the process, enabled them to identify and clarify the quality of feelings that were emerging and the more intimate kinds of relationship they were seeking. As Sam later said, "At first we just wanted the club so we could learn to do things, but now it's more than that, we're learning about ourselves".

The Frame of Reference — The Family:

As the character of group life becomes increasingly intimate, there are indications that the frame of reference for the experience becomes a familial one. References to siblings are more prevalent — "You remind me of my punk brother when you do that", says Jack, giving Sam an elbow in the ribs after Sam adds up the food expenses more quickly than he can. The worker may be referred to, often jokingly, as the "Club Mama" or "Pop". Discussions about what goes on at home tend to become more revealing, more emotionally charged and of longer duration than previously. Direct conscious parallels between group and family life are somewhat drawn. As these paragraphs are being written, we are looking at a large sheet of paper which the leader of a coeducational group of twelve year olds brought in from last week's meeting. This group has been through two years of activity and summer camp together, with considerable work on "separating the boys from the girls". Now, one member, Karen, reflecting on what the club is like, takes a big sheet of newsprint and on one side, prints with water color the names of the camp director and his wife, followed by the names of their children. On the other side of the sheet, she prints in similar manner the group worker's name followed by the names of the other children. While we cannot assume that this kind of production from Karen, who, incidentally, is a bright, reality-oriented youngster, means that the social work group members literally think their clubs are families, it is true that references to the fact that clubs have family-like qualities appear with increasing frequency through conversation and action during this intimate phase. Thus, as the worker permits dependency, closeness and high involvement, the group experience tends to be perceived in a light that is a reflection of family experience.

Credence is added to the family frame-of-reference hypothesis by the appearance in some instance of transference reactions. It is often not easy to state with certainty, of course, whether a piece of behavior in a group merits the transference appellation in the classical sense, or should be labeled simply as "life style", or "indigenous" to the current situation. It is also true that members possessing healthier psyches are able to move closer to their peers and leaders without manifesting inappropriate behavior. Nevertheless, it does appear that, even with normal persons, where permission is given by the worker, patterns of behavior and perception tend to reflect quite closely family backgrounds and experience. In this sense, where group members are permitted to bring a significant part of themselves into the group and to determine the character of the experience in relation to the safe, non-retaliatory framework initially set up by the worker, transference would seem to be one very natural outcome.

Worker Focus:

In this context, decisions must be made by the worker as to how much and what kind of structure he will introduce, how much "personal" material he will encourage, and how he will deal with this material. Structuring, through selective use of activities, timing and manipulation of programming and the way in which the worker responds to the personal material, determine to a large extent "What comes out". Group record analysis suggests that group composition and individual need will also influence the amount of pressure from members for uncovering. In general, direct confrontation and clarification in social work groups in relation to this family-like intimacy will be done within the confines of the current group experience. In this sense, transference is dealt with in terms of its derivatives, as evidence in feelings and reactions to the here and now. Thus, the client uses the group as a practice situation in the service of ego-building.

We have noted that often the process of clarification during stage three takes place not only in relation to specific attitudes and emotions, but finds expression also in the general meaning of the group experience. Significantly, discussion of "what this club is all about" occurs typically in response to or as a culmination of an inter-personal crisis. The membership crisis, for example, which occurs during the power struggle stage, may reappear during stage three when one of the members brings a friend to a meeting and proposes that he be voted in. In the jockeying for votes, in the initiatory rites that are proposed, in the antagonisms toward and the support for this prospective addition, in threats to quit the club if he gets in, may be seen reflections of the meaning of the group to the members. In observing the emotional upheaval and the regression that even normal groups sometimes exhibit at times like this, one is reminded of the mixed pleasure and pain occasioned in a family by the birth of a new brother or sister. And in the course of figuring out whether "this guy deserves to belong to the club", group members often state quite eloquently the goals of the group and describe the present condition of their mutual relationship: "He wouldn't be comfortable if he came in now; he wouldn't know all about the things we've done together". "Maybe the club would be too crowded and there wouldn't be enough stuff to go around". "You brought your friend in, why can't I bring mine in?" "I think we should vote her in, after all isn't the club to help you make friends?"

Stage 4. Differentiation

The stage of differentiation is one in which members begin to accept one another as distinct individuals, to see the social worker as a unique person and to see this group experience as a unique experience from which each can find an acceptable intra-psychic equilibrium. As clarification of power-relationships gave freedom for autonomy and intimacy, so clarification of and coming to terms with intimacy and mutual acceptance of personal needs brings the freedom and the ability to differentiate, and to evaluate relationships and events in the group on a reality basis.

The identification of "what the club is for", as illustrated above, seems almost to be the signal that differentiation is around the corner. As the members consider the nature and meaning of the group, there is a tendency for them to reflect consciously on how it compares with the other groups and social situations with which they are acquainted. We have noticed how this process of comparison comes after intimate relationships have been entered into and as a culmination of a struggle over deviance and conformity, sibling-like rivalry and interdependence. We see emerging a new acceptance of individual differences and group permission for free expression in this regard. If interdependence has been accepted, there is also the emergence of a group system for *Mutual support* for this individuality, and, where needed, consistent controls when individual behavior becomes group-destructive. The "Valiants", described above, as they emerged from stage three, developed such a system in relation to George's problem with arithmetic.

When it first became evident that George was having a lot of trouble figuring bowling scores, the boys had ignored or glossed over the problem, keeping score for him or turning over helping functions to the worker. Later George's unwillingness to relate to the others or to "open up" became equated with this "stupidity" and he was ridiculed and berated for it. The other boys became very impatient with his slowness in game-scoring and change-making, and would take over his duties or grab money from him and disdainfully do his figuring for him. As mutual acceptance of school and relationship problems grew along with a new sense of responsibility for one another, the members began to wait quite patiently for George even if the game were slowed down, but refused his attempts to get them to give him the answers. They also refused to let him avoid planning discussions, saying, "How can we plan without you?"

The cohesion that appears in stage four when based on the recognition of individuals' needs and prerogatives, mutual identification and high communication, tends to assume a flexible character. Although more organization for work and play is possible than previously, role systems and status hierarchies tend to be less rigid.

The "Macs", a group of teenage boys, had always permitted Ernie to be in charge of their baseball games. Attempts by Kevin to assume leadership were squashed or resulted in formation of two distinct sub-groups playing separate games. Gradually, as the boys became aware of one another's strengths and weaknesses, and with support and protection from the worker, they began to feel safer about expressing individual needs. Role challenge also could be faced without divisive flight as previously had been the case. When Kevin at this point again asserted his leadership, he gained support and Ernie was able to accept the idea of himself and Kevin taking turns leading the games with the whole group participating together.

Related to the emergence of shared leadership is the growth of functional roles. We note, for example, the girl in the adolescent group who is not able to take leadership in initially contacting a boy's club, but is recognized by the girls as the "boss" when they are preparing a buffet for a party. There are obvious implications in this process for the development of the freedom to accept and experiment with alternative modes of behavior.

Power problems during the differentiative stage tend to be minimized, and decision making and control efforts are settled more often by recourse to the objective facts and to mutual contracts that have been established.

It is our feeling that cohesion, as described here, arrived at after other development problems have been worked through, avoids having what some group therapists have termed a "counter-therapeutic effect".[23] This is not to ignore the difference in goals and techniques between ego-supportive and intensive psychotherapy groups; they do necessitate perhaps different degrees of "groupiness". What is important is that, even in a therapeutically oriented social work group, cohesion not be regarded by workers as something which can only be purchased at the expense of individual integrity. It can be a product of an experience in which individual autonomy has been nurtured.[24] It may, in fact, be employed as a

---

[23] Slavson, for example, conceives of the therapeutic groups as a "compresence of patients (individuals) rather than a closely knit group, and feels that any pressure for conformity that is exerted on the patient through the emergency of "we" feeling or through the development of group goals, inhibits the patient's freedom of expression. He emphasizes, similar rather than common aims and inter-stimulation rather than "so-called interaction". Slavon, *Op. Cit.,* pp. 20–21.

[24] Benne points out how interdependence need not destroy personal autonomy and argues eloquently for the contribution which democratic groups can make to the enhancement of individuality. Benne, Kenneth D. 'The Use of Fraternity", *Daedalus,* Spring, 1961, pp. 233–246.

tool for supporting growth on the social level and promoting the continued meeting of individual needs through the mutually agreed upon social contract. By the same token, group workers must reflect on how often they try to induce cohesion in response to agency or community needs, or in an attempt promote growth *before* the members have reached a point where they are willing and able to enter into such a binding contract. A familiar example of this induction process is the use of a camping trip to promote interdependence and cohesion within a newly formed group. With supplies limited to what can be toted to the isolated camp site and with primitive survival conditions, cohesion and working for the good of all are absolute necessities. It is our contention that even if such a venture may be carried off with relative smoothness (sharing food and supplies, splitting up chores, etc.), there is considerable likelihood that some potentially unhealthy conditions may be created. These are: (1) the worker (and agency) will in effect decide what the values of the club are to be, (2) needs of the group must take precedence over needs of the individual and (3) the club is manipulated into acting like a mature group regardless of whether the members have had a chance to explore freely what kind of social contract they will enter into together.

Identity and the Internal Frame of Reference:
The appearance of cohesion and the ability to differentiate is accompanied by a heightened sense of group and individual identity. Perceptions of the worker and the other members tend to be more appropriate and less influenced by prior associations (i.e., parents and siblings). Where references such as "You remind me of my brat sister" are made, they tend to be accompanied by the recognition that, although similarities exist between "home" and the club, the latter is nevertheless a new and distinct experience. References to "our social worker" tend to be numerous. Club program acquires customs and traditional ways of operating (e.g., "We always take a break and play a game of dodge ball after our business meeting"), club names or insignia and organizational structures, (i.e., officers, dues, attendance rules, etc.) tend to reflect the character and history of the particular group more closely than those adopted during early meetings. Cooperative planning and sustained activity (as has been noted in many descriptions of the "good group") are more prevalent. There is also less need for

constant activity as a vehicle for enabling interaction. We find, for instance, that groups may at times engage in no specific program, but prefer to "sit and gab". Incidentally, this occurs even in latency age groups, who are not traditionally seen as being able to carry on sustained conversation with a professional adult present.

Relating to the *community* and to *other groups* now becomes a more natural and comfortable process. More secure in their own relationship together and in the identity of their group, members typically become interested in meeting other groups through sports competition, coed parties and the like, or by sharing a camping experience or working together on a project. Trips in the community tend to be less fraught with conflict and acting out. Projects in relation to the agency or community (e.g., constructing a booth for the Center Purim Carnival, selling tickets for a Red Feather dance, doing a neighborhood cleanup) now serve to strengthen group identity and enhance individual feelings of self-worth, whereas earlier attempts of this type might have imposed severe strains on club organization and on individual willingness to give.

As we have implied, the group experience achieves a *functionally autonomous* character in stage four. In freeing perceptions of the group situation from distortions of extraneous experience and in creating its unique institutions and mores, the group becomes, in a sense, its own frame of reference. Group events tend to be evaluated and reactions related to this *internal frame of reference.* "Hey, Georgia (new member), don't kick Alice's skates like that. She's just a slow skater and you clobberin' her won't do her any good; besides, we don't settle fights by hittin' each other . . ."

Worker Focus:

The worker's activity during stage four most appropriately centers around clarification and facilitation of differentiative and cohesive processes. If development has proceeded naturally up to this point, he may concentrate principally on letting the group run itself. He may assume more of a resource-person role — giving information regarding trips or recreational facilities in the community, arranging for lending of tools so the group can build a bridge at their camp site, establishing contact with other agencies, etc. The worker's role in facilitating evaluation of "What's going on" remains an important function as it was earlier. Clarification in relation to group identity (What is this club like, how is it different from other

56

clubs, how did we get this way), and interdependence (We're interested in each other now, we really know one another, we've been through a lot together . . .") are fairly distinctive of stage four.* Also, of great help in firming up the learning and skills achieved by individual members is consideration of "What the club has meant to me, and what changes it has made in the way I perform in and think about social situations." We suspect that it is this latter area of clarification and evaluation that is performed least in groups. Yet, in terms of creating a climate and a contract for using the group as a feed-back vehicle for discussion of extra-group growth and in promoting carry-over during the subsequent to group experience, it might be a crucially significant venture.

Stage 5. Separation

The fifth stage is that of separation. The group experience has been completed and members may begin to move apart and find new resources for meeting social, recreational and vocational needs. The process of termination in this stage may involve some regression and recapitulation, both spoken and acted out, of former group experiences and relationship patterns. In addition to permitting of anxiety over separation and loss, the recapitulation serves an evaluating function, helping the group to re-think and assess the meaning and value of the total experience. If the group experience has made a significant impact on the group members, the assumption is that it now becomes the frame of reference for approaching new social, group and familial situations.

The approach of group termination appears to set off a number of reactions, the diversity of which is reminiscent of the range of approach-avoidance maneuvers displayed in Stage 1. Anxiety over coming together that was experienced in earlier stages, now is felt in relation to moving apart and breaking bonds that have been formed. Even where individual contacts among members or between members and worker antedate or continue subsequent to

---

*We noted after listing these quotations, how reminiscent in theme they were of the four questions asked by Jews on Passover Eve. It appears that in the process of establishing an identity, whether on an individual, small group, or national level, similar processes are at work and reflected in both the informal, discourse and ceremonial observances of those involved.

group association, there is a significant impact of finality that is evident in records and recollections of group terminations. The following basic reactions have been observed repeatedly in groups which were in the process of termination. They are the devices typically employed by members to avoid and forestall terminating, on the one hand, and to face and accomplish it, on the other.

(a) Denial:

(1) Simple denial — where members simply "forget" the worker's telling them when the club would end. They are completely surprised and sometimes profess to have been "tricked" when the final four or five meetings roll around. Often, after apparently accepting the fact of the group's ending with the conclusion of the program year members will ask, "We'll begin again next year, won't we?"

(2) Clustering — where members band together, as if in protection against the chill and loneliness of separation. Sometimes this takes the form of "super-cohesion" which may even be expressed in direct physical drawing together. The following record excerpt provided the label for this phenomenon.

> . . . (As the group headed homeward from a long sight-seeing drive), Chester opened up the area of termination again — I stated simply that the group was going to terminate this year and that they would not be meeting as a club in the fall although they would be going to the (Agency) camp. As I started to explain why the group would not be meeting, the boys clustered around me in the car, the two in the front seat sliding over very close to me, and the ones in the back seats coming up and almost leaning over me, their heads all bunched together around my shoulders.

(b) Regression:

(1) Simple disorganized regression — where there is a sliding backward in ability to cope with interpersonal and organizational tasks, usually accompanied by outbursts of anger toward one another and the worker and toward the idea of the club ending. Quarrels that were previously settled tend to reappear and individual and group demands for dependence on the leader increase.

(2) The regressive fugue — where members begin behaving in a manner that is dramatically reminiscent of earlier developmental

stages. This condition, more extreme than the recapitulative reenactment to be described next, reflects a desire to "begin all over again" and involves a phantasy-like detachment from the here and now of the group. The following material, taken from the records of an adolescent group in its final month, illustrates an extreme form that this wish-fulfilling detachment may take.

> (On the way to the bowling alley) . . . Peter suddenly expressed the wish that we could begin all over again, and quite suddenly the group reverted back to the very beginning of the club. Joey, who was sitting beside me suddenly called me "Shep" (the name of the worker who started the group two years ago) asking, "Shep" where he was taking them. Chester picked this up by asking what kind of a club this is and what we are going to do today. Other members pointed out the direction of the Neighborhood House, and pointed out local things in the neighborhood . . . (they asked) about Shep's position at the agency. Suddenly, the conversation shifted back to "Fred" (my name) and they began reminiscing about all the things we have done together —.

(c) We Still Need the Club:
Where members have seen the group experience as a helping one, there is a tendency to feel that the group will somehow continue if the worker sees that they still need his service. The following excerpts are taken from the record of one of the last meetings of the Deuces, a group of young adolescent boys. The Deuces had been outcasts from the local neighborhood house because of their stealing and anti-social behavior. During three years with a detached worker they had gradually given up their delinquent behavior and had been taken back into the center.

> As we were discussing the club ending, Sharky said in a very loud voice to the other boys, "Well, fellas, it's down to the square tonight for a nice haul." The boys picked up on this and hinted broadly about how much "loot" they planned to lift when they broke into some nearby stores that evening. With forced gaiety, they elaborated on their plans saying, "Then we can steal a car and get picked up — that'll show Herbie (worker) — we really need the club . . ."

(Later at the agency summer camp) Sharky led the other boys in an orgy of petty theft and defiance of counselors. This ended in a tearful session with the camp director, Sharky dejectedly stating that he knew they'd "all end up in jail . . ."

As indicated in this material, speech and action to show us the desire for continuation of service is very noticeable in groups which are problem-focused (e.g., delinquency, physical handicap, emotional disturbance, social isolation, etc.). Quite typically, these concerns are reflected in questions such as: "How far have we come — are we ready to move on our own?" The Deuces show their despair, feeling of loss and fear of back-sliding. Evidence suggests, however, that similar concerns are voiced, albeit with less desperation, in more normal, growth-oriented groups as well. On the surface, this attempt to prove, "We still need the club", has manipulative characteristics and members often state quite frankly their intent in putting on a display of regression or making pleas for help with problems. This may reflect awareness on the member's parts of the kinds of problems that intrigue the worker and the suspicion that, "If we grow up he won't be interested in us anymore."

(d) Recapitulation:

(1) Reenactment — a phenomenon at times regressive in character, where earlier modes of interaction, developmental crises, and program events are relived. It is not uncommon to see members requesting to repeat the activity they did on "The first day of the club." This reenactment is quite often accomplished by discussion of minute details of the events — what games were played, who arrived first, what the leader said, etc.

(2) Review — very closely related to the active recepitulation of group experiences. This is a more conscious process of reminiscing about club life and events.

> . . . (They reminisced) with me about the things they did together, the fun they had, some of the hard times, some of the trouble that members had gotten into, places they had been, and how much bigger they are now compared to when the club began. (Then they) . . . shifted into the area of behavior, with some saying that they don't do some of the things they used to, like stealing, breaking into the Neighborhood House, having the cops chase them.

(e) Evaluation:

Evaluation is typically quite closely tied to the reenacting phase of recapitulation. If the first trip to the amusement park that the group took, for example, is repeated during the final period of the group, members typically reflect on how much "like the first time" it is and then discover "how long ago it seems" and "how far we've come." Thus the process of repeating earlier events or relational states, in addition to serving the need to recapture an experience that is slipping away, also may become part of the process of evaluating the meaning and worth of the experience.

Very often, review *follows* recapitulation and reflects a more rationalized and organized experience. Review and evaluation typically continue throughout the period of separation, and may also take place subsequent to termination of regular meetings. We discovered it happening through individual contacts among members and with the worker, at agency camps, and, quite significantly, at group reunions, even a year or more after termination.

(f) Flight:

(1) Nihilistic flight — the destructive reaction to separation. There is a denial of the positive meaning of the experience, and attempts are made to control the grief of separation and (phantasied) desertion, by aggressive action. There is also an attempt to prove that the worker and agency either didn't care for them in the first place or are terminating the group in retaliation for bad behavior. To this end, members exhibit a variety of rejecting and rejection-provoking behaviors. These include such things as missing meetings, quitting the group a month before termination, being directly hostile to other members and worker with accompanying challenges to "bounce me", sabotaging planning and program events, and pointing out "better" clubs or activities that they are "more interested in". The feelings that accompany and underly these actions are revealed in such statements as: 'I guess you couldn't stand us any longer". "Will we be glad to get rid of you!" (Note that double meaning there) "I'll never get tangled up with anyone like you (worker) again." "I'm glad it's going to be over — this is nothing but a club for queers, anyway." "We're gonna burn this goddam' place down before we go." (All literal quotations.)

(2) Positive flight — where constructive moves are made toward "self-weaning" from the group. This includes finding new

groups, activities, work interests, friends, etc., outside the group while continuing as a member. The new contacts, which may be started well in advance of termination, serve to substitute for interests and gratifications which will no longer be fulfilled after the group's end. They also represent a broadening and maturing of interests and skills. Familiar examples of this process are: increased use of agency and community resources (other agency clubs, lounge programs, public recreational facilities, civic groups, etc.), getting part-time jobs or doing vocational planning, making new individual friendships with peers and adults, and increased physical mobility.

A few general comments are appropriate concerning the reaction-coping devices described above. In the first place, we discover that all of the reactions tend to occur — with modifications in intensity and duration — in most groups which have continued with sustained attendance over a significant period of time (at least a year). Secondly, unlike the major developmental stages, there is more of a tendency for the various separation reactions to occur in flashes and in clusters. We have observed on occasion, for example, all of the five reactions occurring within the space of an hour during one group meeting. Third, although we can see certain progression in relationality among reactions (e.g., regression-recapitulation — review — evaluation), their actual emergence is not always in sequential fashion. As a matter of fact, it is not at all uncommon for group members to evaluate their experience together in a logical, reflective manner one week, and at the following meeting explode into an orgy of mutual recrimination over who's been "causing all the fights for the past year", or lead the worker on a hide-and-seek chase through the agency building.

Program:

In the stage of separation, program tends to reflect the general dynamic characteristics of the stage, in that there is some regressive breakdown at times, desire for repetition of earlier program activities, and an increase in activities having an out-group and high-mobility focus. As a reaffirmation of the meaning of the club experience, we see big events being planned, with the "last big blowout" sometimes assuming a rather destructive character (viz. the difference between constructive and nihilistic flight). Side by side with "super-cohesive" final program (e.g., week-end outing, dances and dinner parties, etc.) we note the reemergence of individually oriented activities —

in one group, model airplanes are requested for the last meeting — in another each girl brings her own sewing project. It is interesting that quite often, as groups sit for a last crafts session, each member working separately, the conversation assumes a nostalgic tone as club experiences are recalled. In older adolescent groups the process of separation is immediately meaningful in terms of preparation for education away from home, vocational training or full-time employment. Visits to schools, factories, employment offices, talks from the worker are frequent program events in this transition. For both older and younger group., the trip into the community at this stage assumes a special significance because of the moving out and new contacts that it implies.

A very mundane but ever-present problem with which groups must contend especially during the final period of group life, is that of program activity becoming stale and monotonous. (We are leaving out the problem of the worker's boredom when the group plays basketball seven meetings in a row.) "You think of something." "We never do nothin' in this club." "What, baking brownie's again?" "We've been to the Museum three times already." "I know we used to play kick-ball, but it's too easy; it's a baby game." "I think I'll sell newspapers next week." These are all familiar attempts illustrating the condition. Activity *ennui* in stages four and five may reflect one or more of four basic problems:

1. Simple lack of new ideas — group and worker must explore new variations, activities, new resources, and open up new creative outlets.
2. Resistance — particularly, in stage five a reaction to the worker's impending withdrawal and the "end of good times together."
3. Program lagging behind group development — the activity that was difficult to master and cooperate on six months ago, now no longer presents a challenge and needs to be replaced, or brought up to date.
4. Separation has been completed — the group has run its course, and attempting to continue activity assumes a post-mortem quality.

Worker Focus:

The worker's activity should be generally oriented once again to facilitating the completion of the major developmental task at hand — in this case, moving apart. To this end, the worker will make opportunities and resources available for individual and group mobility. Whether through group discussion of extra-group or post-group activities and interests, or helping to establish new contacts, he indicates the availability of these gratifying outlets for growth and his confidence in members' abilities to use them. The worker's focus on facilitating evaluation should be typically heavier during this period than previously. His work should be shaped by the recapitulative character of group behavior. The most delicate part of his work in effecting the separation may be in the area of helping members to express (through activity and verbally) and come to terms with the ambivalence that is involved in termination. If this is done, there will be a greater likelihood that the positive learning of the group experience may be freely transferred to new social situations. It is possible that group workers have too often assumed that relationships developed with clients in group meetings, being "not as intensive" as those in individual work, are easier to terminate. When we fail to recognize the impact that the group experience and its attendant relationships have on individuals, we tend to minimize and deny feelings of loss that the members and we ourselves have when it is time to part. Thus, in helping the group to move out the worker must be sensitive to the seriousness of "letting go" even as he is helping the group members to muster the strength to seek new experiences. Also, as the worker indicates his post-group availability for individual contact (e.g., job referral, attending a school graduation. conferring with parents, dropping in for a "friendly chat,") he helps the members to tie their group experiences more directly to their subsequent life experiences. This process may prevent the positive group experience from being idealized as a "great time" only and unrelated to what happens later on the "outside". We must consider the possibility also that continuing support in varying forms and with varying degrees of frequency for both individuals and groups over extended periods of time may often be a necessary part of our commitment in providing meaningful help.

Below is a summary chart of the five stages and their major dimensions.

MODEL FOR STAGE OF GROUP DEVELOPMENT

STAGE	DYNAMIC CHARACTERISTIC	FRAME OF REFERENCE	PROGRAM	WORKER FOCUS
1. Pre-Affiliation	Exploration	SOCIETAL "The Crafts Class" "Teacher" "Coach" "Hey Kid"	Quick Satisfaction Important	Allowing and Supporting Distance
	Approach-Avoidance Dilemma		Parallel Individual Play	Inviting Trust Gently
	Stereotypic Activity		Exploring Ambivalence Between Cooperation & Cleanup vs. Hit & Run	Facilitating Exploration
	Trust, Preliminary Commitment		Ambivalence Over Accepting Material	Providing Program Structure & Initiation
			Non-Giving to Group	
2. Power & Control	Locking Horns with the Reality of the Group	TRANSITIONAL "How come you let him get away with that?"	Program Breakdown At Time, Low Planning	Permitting Rebellion
	Status Jockeying		Aggressive Competition	Protecting Safety of Individuals and Property
	Power Struggles Among Members and with Worker		Testing Strength and Authority	Providing Activities for Mastery
	Autonomy, Individual and Group		Attempts at Formalizing Relationships through Dues, Rules	Clarification of Power Struggle
	Drop Out Danger High			
	Normative & Membership Crises Begin			

STAGE	DYNAMIC CHARACTERISTIC	FRAME OF REFERENCE	PROGRAM	WORKER FOCUS
3. Intimacy	Normative & Membership Crises Continue Mutual Revelation Dependency Intensified Interpersonal Involvement Transference Facing "What this club is for".	FAMILIAL "You're a good club Mama". "You're worse than my little sister".	Activity Openly Emotion-Laden, Struggles for Attention & Material Growing Ability to Plan, Carry Out Group Projects, but Often with Emotional Turmoil	Consistent Giving in Face of Turmoil Flexible Assumption or Giving of Responsibility as Group Vacillates Clarification of Feelings, Positive & Negative
4. Differentiation	Cohesion Free Expression Mutual Support High Communication Few Power Problems Identity	GROUP – INTERNAL "Our Social Worker" "This club is Different"	Freer Mutual Giving Club Traditions & Customs Around Activities Cooperative Activity Planned, Sustained Projects, etc. in Relationship to Community, Other Groups Outside Interests Start	Helping Group to Run Itself Facilitating Opportunities to Act as a Unit in re Other Groups and Community Facilitating Evaluation Process

MODEL FOR STAGE OF GROUP DEVELOPMENT *continued*

STAGE	DYNAMIC CHARACTERISTIC	FRAME OF REFERENCE	PROGRAM	WORKER FOCUS
5. Separation	Denial Regression and Recapitulation	GROUP (Carried to other Social Situations new groups)	High Mobility, Travel	Letting Go
	Review and Evaluation		Problem of Activity Routine Becoming Stale	Concentrating on Group and Individual Mobility
	Moving Apart, Nihilistic and Positive Flight		Re-Enacting Stage One Activities	Facilitating
			Outside Interests – Vocational in Older Groups	Evaluation
			Reunion	Facilitating Post-Grp. Meeting of Needs via Other Resources

V. CONCLUSIONS

We have presented the outlines as we see them of the five general stages of group development. Much more could be said about the implications of our model for diagnosis of individual and group behavior, and handling. We have, for example, limited our discussion of individual diagnosis primarily to stage one. In this connection, we have appended below several questions which merit further study. As it stands now, we believe the model provides practical and useful guidelines in three principal areas. They are: (1) Diagnosis of individual behavior in groups — the manner in which the individual member reacts with others, how he responds to the unfolding group developmental tasks, and the rapidity with which he masters these tasks, (2) Understanding of group behavior in terms of how developmental tasks are met and resolved, and (3) Intervention — the action of the worker as an enabler, providing program tools, clarification, protection, support, etc., to the group in relation to developmental tasks. It remains for practitioners to test the model and the theory it embodies against their own working experience and to decide whether and in what ways it answers questions or provides useful directions for action. We consider the model to be a beginning. If, in the process of application to various settings, it arouses curiosity and further investigation, or disagreement, and a search for more valid and useful alternative schemes, it will have served a worthwhile purpose.

VI. PERTINENT CLINICAL — THEORETICAL PROBLEMS REQUIRING FURTHER STUDY

There are a number of important questions regarding the validity and applicability of the Stage Model which bear further thought and study, as well as some areas which require further elaboration in order for the Model to be a more useful tool for practice.

1. Duration of Stages:
Investigation indicates that different groups progress through developmental stages at different rates of speed. It is possible to

identify "average" rates of speed for various types of groups (i.e., according to age, levels of members' personality adjustment, group purpose, etc.)?

2. *Differential Growth Rates Among Members:*

Some children progress more rapidly than others. What are the implications here for group composition? Do "fast movers" pull slower peers along; do "slow movers" retard group development?

3. *Adding New Members:*

If we view the group experience as having a "life cycle", what does it mean to add a new member, particularly subsequent to the formative phase? Will he "catch up?" Will his addition create a harmful pause in group development, or a helpful opportunity for evaluation? Does it make a difference as to when a new member is added?

4. *Orderly Progress vs. Circularity:*

We have evidence to suggest that past group growth problems tend to be reenacted during transitional periods (e.g., an approach-avoidance conflict triggered off by emergence of stage three intimacy). Does this mean that stages may have a circular character rather than a straight-line developmental one? Or does it mean that the major stage characteristics as outlined here still hold true, but need some slight modification in terms of circularity or regression, especially during transitional periods?

5. *Relationship Between Age of Group Members and Relative Importance of Developmental Issues:*

There is evidence that suggests that different age groups react differently to group developmental problems as they arise. The possibility also exists that certain issues may be responded to and handled in different sequence. For instance, the power struggle between the worker and the group in adolescent groups appears early and occupies a great deal of time and attention. (A reflection of the struggle for autonomy that they are going through with parents and society). Conversely, we have noted that in latency age groups there tends to be more of a concern, especially during early phases, as to whom the worker likes best, and that vying for the worker's attention pre-dates member solidarity.

6. Similarities Between Group Developmental Stages and Individual Growth Stages:

We have mentioned some of the interesting similarities between group stages and individual growth stages as proposed by Erikson (1950). Is there any causal relationship involved in this similarity? How can similarities, causal or coincidental, be capitalized on for the purpose of enhancing growth?

7. Program Analysis:

We need a better understanding of the intrinsic qualities of various program media and their manipulation as they related to the working through of developmental problems at various points in a club's development.

8. Worker Technique:

We have given here only the broadest generalization regarding the worker's differential responses during various developmental phases. This area needs to be greatly elaborated and specific techniques defined and evaluated.

REFERENCES

AUSTIN, DAVID, "Goals for Gang Workers", *Social Work,* Vol. 2, No. 4, October, 1957, pp. 43–50.

BENNE, KENNETH D., "The Uses of Fraternity", *Daedulus,* Spring, 1961, pp. 233–246.

BENNIS, WARREN G. & SHEPARD, H. A., "A Theory of Group Dynamics", *Human Relations,* Vol. 9, No. 4, 1956, pp. 415–457.

BERNSTEIN, SAUL, "Charting Group Progress", in *Readings in Group Work,* Dorothea Sullivan, ed., Association Press, 1952.

—— "Conflict in Group Work" (Mimeographed) Boston University School of Social Work, Boston, Massachusetts.

CHIN, ROBERT, "The Utility of System Models and Developmental Modes for Practitioners", *The Planning of Change,* Bennis, Warren G., Kenneth D. Benne and Robert Chin, ed., New York: Holt, Rinehart and Winston, 1961.

ERIKSON, ERIC H., *Childhood and Society,* New York: Norton, 1950.

FOLLETT, MARY P., Creative Experience, New York: Longmans, Green and Co., 1924.

FREY, LOUISE A., "Support and the Group: A Generic Treatment Form", *Social Work,* Vol. 7, No. 4, October, 1962, pp. 35–40.

GRACE, PRISCILLA B., "A Scheme for Differentiating Therapeutic Group Work From Group Psychotherapy". Unpublished Master's Thesis, Boston University School of Social Work, 1960.

HOMANS, GEORGE C., *The Human Group.* New York: Harcourt, Brace & Co., 1950.

KINDLESPERGER, WALTER, "Stages of Group Development", in *The Use of the Group* in Social Welfare Settings (mimeographed). Tulane University School of Social Work, New Orleans, 1957, pp. 8–9.

MAIER, HENRY W., and ASSOCIATES, Research Projection Group Development, 1961–62, University of Washington, School of Social Work, Seattle.

MANN, JAMES, "An Analytically Oriented Study of Groups", *Journal of Psychiatric Social Work,* Vol. 20, No. 4, June, 1951, pp. 137–143.

—— "Some Theoretic Concepts of the Group Process", *The International Journal of Group Psychotherapy,* Vol. 5, No. 3, July, 1955, pp. 235–251.

NORTHEN, HELEN, "Social Group Work: A Tool for Changing Behavior of Disturbed Acting-Out Adolescents", in *Social Work With Groups,* 1958, New York: National Association of Social Workers, 1958.

SCHEIDLINGER, SAUL, "The Concepts of Social Group Work and of Group Psychotherapy", Social Case Work, Vol. 34, No. 7, July, 1953, pp. 292–297.

SCHUTZ, WILLIAM C., "The Interpersonal Underworld", *Harvard Business Review,* Vol. 36, No. 4, July-August, 1958, pp. 123–135.

AEMRAD, ELVIN V., and ARSENIAN, JOHN, "The Use of Group Processes in Teaching Group Dynamics", *American Journal of Psychiatry,* Vol. 108, November, 1951, pp. 358–363.

SLAVSON, S. R., "Common Sources of Error and Confusion in Group Psychotherapy", International Journal of Group Psychotherapy, Vol. 3, No. 1, Jan., 1953, pp. 3–28.

STANDISH, CHRISTOPHER T., and SEMRAD, ELVIN V., "Group Psychotherapy with Psychotics", *Journal of Psychiatric Social Work,* Vol. 20, No. 4, June, 1951, pp. 143–150.

THELEN, HERBERT and DICKERMAN, WATSON, "Stereotypes and the Growth of Groups", *Education Leadership,* Vol. 6, No. 5, Feb., 1949, pp. 309–316.

TRECKER, HARLEIGH, Social Group Work: *Principles and Practices.* New York: Association Press, 1955.

VARON, EDITH, "Group Psychotherapy Transition From the Initial to the Middle Phase". Paper presented at Second Annual Institute of the Northeastern Society for Group Psychotherapy, Boston, April 25, 1958.

Chapter 3

CONFLICT AND GROUP WORK

Saul Bernstein

Conflict is pervasive in human affairs and it is generously present in groups. As individuals form and join groups, their values, goals and interests inevitably vary. Differences arise not only from intra-psychic sources, but also from stages of development,* roles, reference groups and other factors. It is almost as inevitable that when groups are served by social agencies new dimensions of differences are added through the presence of the worker and the agency. It is also true that some of these differences will take the form of conflict (to be characterized below). Hence, on the basis of its frequency and of its profound implications for groups, conflict commands attention.

The attitudes of the group worker toward conflict can be of varying kinds, which have diverse implications for the nature of his intervention. He may, at one pole, regard conflict as unpleasant and undesirable, and as an indication of immaturity, perhaps even as a reflection of his own inadequacy. This position about conflict is far from rare in our culture. As one example, several volunteer leaders were using charts for assessing progress in groups (Bernstein, 1952). An important variable involved the handling of conflict by the groups. One chart after another was turned in showing no conflict. It seems reasonable to interpret these responses as reflecting more the attitudes of the volunteers toward conflict than the actual absence of it in the groups they led.

Another illustration is provided in a productive book on conflict. In his Preface and Introduction, Coser (1956) delves into the history of American sociology indicating that in its earlier days it was much concerned with conflict as a social process. In more

---

*See preceding article.

72

recent decades, however, he claims that co-operative processes and structure have been given more attention and that conflict has been neglected. Among the various explanations Coser offers is that sociology moved away from identification with social reform toward a somewhat neutral scientific position in relation to social change, with the added recent component of working for industry and government. Perhaps it is not intellectually frivolous to suggest that this trend in sociology away from emphasizing conflict is indicative of large components of what has occurred in our society.

Social work seems to present a mixed picture in relation to conflict. On the one hand, it has been heavily influenced by Freudian psychology, which makes conflict a central construct in the understanding of how people develop, feel and act. In fact, according to this theory, people are constantly living in conflict and by their very nature cannot escape it. On the other hand, social work is very much influenced by the general social atmosphere in which conflict tends to be given a place of lesser importance. In terms of values, it may be rated highly negative. As an illustration, in "The Teaching of Values and Ethics in Social Work Education", Mrs. Pumphrey lists words used by her resource people according to whether they were regarded positively or negatively in terms of values. Under the heading "Words Representing Disvalues",[1] conflict appears. Apparently, it was regarded as dysfunctional in relation to social work values.

The worker having this attitude toward conflict may behave in a variety of ways. His concern could be to head off, prevent and even to suppress conflict in groups. This feeling would undoubtedly be conveyed to the members, who might be led to a sense of shame or inadequacy about actions which express conflict or which move toward facing it. Another worker stance could be that conflict is somehow an unfortunate concomitant of this stage in the group's existence, but that this unpleasantness is a temporary evil and real business and living will come just as soon as we can get over this messiness. There may well be other implications for actions by the worker with this point of view about conflict.

At the other pole is the position which venerates conflict as

---

[1] Pumphrey, Muriel. "The Teaching of Values and Ethics in Social Work Education", Volume XIII, Curriculum Study, Council on Social Work Education, 1959, Appendix D, p. 143.

almost an ideal state. There is something of this quality in Coser's book. He sees conflict as having many contributions to make to maintaining and elaborating the group as a social system. Others emphasize the free expression of aggressive feelings in groups, which is apt to lead to conflict. Basic to this position is the idea that conflict is close to the final stuff out of which a good — or not so bad life — can or must be made. In the context of this point of view, conflict will be stimulated and apparently it is not too difficult to do this kind of stimulation. Group workers, however, do not seem to have fallen into this position.

A third — and final for this article — stance in relation to conflict is that it has its terrors but that it frequently offers magnificent opportunities for growth. While one may or may not agree with the position that growth can take place only through conflict, the latter does have rich potentials. There is nothing automatically beneficial about conflict. In fact, it can be highly destructive, producing retrogression and brutality. But, if it is handled thoughtfully and skillfully, it can result in highly constructive change. Perhaps the most important goal is not so much the outcome of any specific situation as is the development of the ability to deal with conflict on a more mature level.

All of the above positions are influenced by what one regards as the nature of man and of society and the values involved. This is not the place to go into a lengthy exposition of social work values. Just a few need to be indicated here. Human worth, with its rich ramifications, is central and basic. Conflict which results in the crushing of this verity in some people in the cause of the aggrandizement of others is a violation. Reciprocity of relationships on relatively similar levels is ideally required, recognizing that many specific and hard realities may interfere. Social workers are often forced by circumstances to set limited goals. In dealing with conflict this may mean that for good diagnostic reasons, satisfaction is felt by the professional when one party shows just a bit of aggression, even if in others this behavior would be regarded as retrogression. Recognizing the potency of such realities, there need nevertheless to be clear, long range directions about the potentials in practically all people to be a good deal more than they apparently are.

Rationality is a core value with many implications for conflict. This is not to say that all or any of us are in fact completely or largely rational. We learned long ago about the powerful forces in individuals and in society which lead us to behave, think and feel quite unreasonably. Along with these forces, however, are others which actually do or potentially can move us in the direction of rationality. A basic value of social work is to deal with the former in such a way as to maximize the latter. Rationality is one of the firm girders in the structure of dealing with conflict.

When relationships are relatively frozen into dominant-subjugated patterns, as was true for some years of race relations in the United States, conflict may well be the major resource at certain periods in history. In small groups to be sure, a worker can try to guide the dominant individual or clique into more democratic ways of thinking and acting, but even in this context it may be necessary and desirable to encourage the dominated to assert themselves. The worker faces many delicate and complex questions especially of maintaining his relationship with those against whom the rebellion is directed and of anticipating the probable consequences of various approaches. Nevertheless, the essential point here is that conflict, with all its potentials for hurting people, may be the only or the best way in some circumstances to loosen up unfortunate relationships and to help them to move toward our social work values. Immediate risks frequently must be taken in relation to long-range aims.

Much more could be said about values but it seems best to let these points come through the specifics to be discussed below. The general position of this paper is that conflict, often unpleasant and even nasty, is not a final end; that it is pervasive and keep-going in groups and that it has tremendous constructive possibilities if utilized skilfully and thoughtfully.

Characteristics of Conflict

In common usage, the term "conflict" seems to describe unpleasantness, tension, hostility, opposing interests, and much else. A more specific framework is needed. One should not suppose that a precise definition is easily attainable,[2] but certain characteristics seem to be clear.

At least – and usually – two "parties" are involved. It would be confusing to speak of persons because the parties could be

---

[2] See Mack and Snyder "The Analysis of Social Conflict", in *Conflict Resolution,* Vol. I, No. 2, for the complexities of defining of conflict.

intrapsychic as between the id and the superego in the Freudian context, or they could consist of groups or subgroups as is frequently the case in group work. It is clearer to think of whatever and whoever is aligned against whatever and whomever.

The parties are involved in a social process of direct interaction. I am highly critical of the Castro government of Cuba but a conflict does not exist because I have no contact with it. This point holds for much of the griping that goes on in groups. Conflict, as characterized here, requires direct interaction and is a narrower concept than hostility or being critical.

Another essential is that there be a struggle over something that is scarce — there is not apparently enough to go around to satisfy the contending parties. The scarcity may apply to material resources, power, status, or values. Those involved ordinarily assume that what their opponents get they will lose, and vice versa.

The intent of the parties often is to triumph over their opponents through neutralizing, injuring or eliminating them. Perhaps there should be added that persuading the opposite numbers of the merits of one's cause may also be a goal.

Thus we have in a crude form the skeleton of conflict. There are still various and important loose ends. Must the conflict be overt, expressed in action? There have been many situations in which one of the parties did not dare come out into the open. This was true of long periods of race relations in the United States and it often applies in small groups. I regard this as latent rather than actual conflict.

The question of who perceives the conflict is a troubling one. For it to be regarded as existing, should we require that both parties and a somewhat disinterested observer all perceive it? Suppose only one party feels that a conflict pertains? Or only the observer? I lean toward the position that only as the two parties recognize the conflict does one actually exist.

Whether competition is conflict is debatable. One point of view holds that as long as the rules of the game, as in athletics, are obeyed, there is no conflict. When players begin to fight or in other ways depart from institutionally prescribed behavior, we then have conflict. A strong case can be made to the contrary. Athletic, and other kinds of competition, involve parties contending for something that is scarce, i.e., both cannot win and one party must be frustrated by the outcome. There is not enough pie to be divided so that both can be satisfied.

76

Without going further into these complexities, the above would seem to provide a beginning framework for a closer examination of conflict. In this connection, it is helpful to turn to Coser's *"The Functions of Social Conflict."* (ibid.) Coser used as a base George Simmel's *Conflict* and rounded out Simmel's ideas by the use of more recent thinking in various fields. A series of propositions is presented in the book. I shall select from Coser those which seem to have the greatest meaning for group work, not following his sequence.

In his "Proposition 3" (ibid., pp. 48–55), Coser makes a distinction between realistic and nonrealistic conflict. Realistic ones "arise from frustration of specific demands within the relationship and from estimates of gains" by each of the parties, involving a "specific result" or issue. A clear illustration is a strike on the part of a labor union for higher wages and a shorter work day. The issues are relatively clear and objective and do not arise primarily from how individual labor leaders feel about individuals in management positions or vice versa, although, of course, feelings get generated. In the context of group work, examples are the struggles for leadership between two or more members, opposed points of view about what to do with the club's treasury, and head on collisions about the selection of activities.

The further point is made by Coser that realistic conflict offers "functional alternatives as to means". To cite a labor situation, action could take the form of negotiation, arbitration, a strike, etc. The end is relatively fixed, but the means is selected in terms of the strategic assessment of what is apt to be most effective in reaching the end. In groups, contenders for leadership can use such means as physical force, bribery, making helpful suggestions, elections, etc.

Non-realistic conflicts do not arise from rival ends or clear issues. They are generated by the need for "tension release" and they may be directed against people with whom there is no issue and who may not have had prior awareness of this kind of feeling in the protagonist. An extreme example is a gang wandering the streets looking for a victim. The gang may fabricate issues, such as that the victim should not walk on this street or that he is of the wrong religion, race or nationality. The primary factor is the need to express aggression. Prejudice is frequently in the non-realistic category, as are many situations in small groups. There are altercations between parties where the issues are very difficult to ascertain and where the rational component is negligible. A striking example from a group record began with a fight between two boys. The loser felt bitterly frustrated and turned around and hit the nearest smaller boy as hard as he could. A similar mechanism is sometimes at work in scapegoating. It may not be safe to vent feelings against the appropriate object and therefore they are directed against a weaker party.

Coser recognizes that the distinction between these two types of conflict involves a "conceptual abstraction from concrete reality in which the two types actually may be merged". What starts as one can easily be extended to include the other. A danger in poorly handled realistic conflict is that feelings can build up to the point where the original issue is submerged or forgotten. He counter-points, however, that there is the temptation in the growing emphasis on human relations to think exclusively in terms of "therapeutic measures" of establishing better relationships, at the cost of recognizing the "real" issues.

The use of the terms "real" and "non-real" by Coser is open to question. It gives higher validity and dignity to economic and political phenomena than it does to psychological ones. The social worker is devoted to the idea that feelings are facts and that they are of great importance. It is difficult indeed to sort out relative weightings to be assigned to wealth, political position, social status and feelings in the precipitation or unfolding of conflict. Neverthe-less, Coser's distinction is a helpful one and it is not easy to find words which maintain it without setting up his reality bias. Perhaps terms like "real issue" and "non-real issue" would come close.

A closely related proposition (No. 4) in Coser's book deals with "conflict and hostile impulses" (ibid., pp. 55–60). Hostility and conflict are related in some ways, but they are far from being identical. Conflict is a social relationship requiring interaction. Hostile impulses and tensions need not involve this immediate inter-action. Parties can be in conflict without hating each other but it has often been found "useful" to hate the opponent, and such feel-ings have been deliberately generated, as in war. An important part of the mediator's function is to help separate the hostility from the issues in real conflict.

There are significant implications for group workers in this proposition. Judgments have to be made as to whether only hostility is involved, and whether it is primarily related to the antagonists or whether such feelings have their origins elsewhere (in family relationships, etc.). These interpretations would have ramifications for what the worker does.

As a sub-unit under his "Proposition 7" (ibid., pp. 73–76), citing MacIver, Simpson and others, Coser deals with communal and non-communal conflict. When the parties are bound together by the common acceptance of basic ends or values and the content and mood of the conflict operate within such assumptions, there is communal conflict. When, on the other hand, the questions at issue are basic ends or values, there is non-communal conflict. An example of the communal type is the approach of American labor. It has, by and large, shared with management the basic aims of the perpetuation and improvement of capitalism and of our form of political democracy. The conflict issues have mainly been on a lesser level, involving increased wages, shorter hours, welfare funds and the like. In some other countries, however, parts of the labor movement have been revolutionary, i.e. they want to change the basic economic and political system.

In small groups, there may be such ideological controversies, but the experience of group workers tends to shift the location of the communal–non-communal question. The point is apt to be whether common values, goals and interests, articulated or just assumed, are meaningful and appealing enough to all to act as a common frame of reference which holds the group together in the face of sharp splits on other issues. It is diagnostically helpful for the group worker to sort out these binding and dividing factors and, at times, to involve the group in this assessment process. Unless both the worker and the group are alert to this dimension, they are apt to encounter some rude shocks as new developments loosen up old bonds.

The temptation is to go on to elaborate on several more of Coser's propositions, but it seems best to mention briefly only a few more:

Proposition 1: (ibid., p. 38)	"Conflict serves to establish and maintain the identities and boundary lines of societies and groups."
	"Conflict with other groups contributes to the establishment and reaffirmation of the identity of the group and maintains its boundaries against the surrounding world."

Proposition 6: (ibid., pp. 67–72)	(paraphrased) In close relationships, hostility may be repressed for a time. When it is expressed in conflict it tends to be more intense than in less personal relationships.
Proposition 8: (ibid., pp. 81–85)	"The absence of conflict cannot be taken as an index of the strength and stability of a relationship. Stable relationships may be characterized by conflicting behavior."
Proposition 16: (ibid., pp. 139–149)	"Struggle brings together otherwise unrelated persons and groups." (For example, many gangs).

The above is a highly selected and segmented version of *The Functions of Social Conflict.* The book merits full and careful reading. The selection was done in relation to group work, which was not at all what Coser had in mind.

A comment is in order about the degree and level of truth of these propositions. They are backed by the insights of scholars and by some evidence. Primarily, however, they are theoretical postulates and therefore group workers should feel free to question and test them. The first step might well be the attempt to grasp sympathetically their significance. It should also be recognized that making such postulates or propositions, even if they should be backed by no evidence in some cases, can provide perceptive insights and theoretical initiatives. Testing by experience and research is essential at some points, but we would lose many valuable ideas if we did not respect and dignify such postulates.

Patterns of Conflict Resolution

Coser and other social scientists may or may not be concerned about the applications of their thinking to practice. We as social workers and group workers are very much concerned about how such ideas can be used helpfully in our work with people. It is to our advantage to take time and give thought to theory which may seem remote from application, but sooner or later we need to return to the compelling and complex demands of our practice and to use it to test theory. This leads directly to questions about what we do with conflict. I shall approach them on two levels. The first is a rather generalized set of patterns of conflict resolution which deals perhaps more with the outcomes or goals than with the methods used by the worker. The second approach goes specifically into diagnosis and action by the worker.

In *Dynamic Administration,* Mary P. Follett (1940) made contributions to thinking about conflict and its resolution. Before turning to her suggestions about resolution, her attitudes toward conflict are worth noting. "I should like to ask you to agree for the moment to think of conflict as neither good nor bad; to consider it without ethical pre-judgment; to think of it not as warfare, but as the appearance of difference, difference of opinions, of interests." (p. 130). "As conflict-difference is here in the world, as we cannot avoid it, we should, I think, use it. Instead of condemning it, we should set it to work for us." (p. 30).

These quotes do not attempt the precision of definition aspired to by Coser and other social scientists, but they do carry the conviction, shared by myself, that conflict, while in itself not a value or a disvalue, presents great opportunities.

Moving into conflict resolution, Miss Follett suggests three patterns: (1) domination, (2) compromise, and (3) integration. Domination is "a victory of one side over the other." It is the "easiest way" temporarily, but in the long run it is not successful. (It is of note that at this point Miss Follett sees the value question in terms of the success or failure in resolving the conflict.)

The second method, compromise, Miss Follett says is the one used to settle most of our conflicts. "Each side gives up a little in order to have peace, or, to speak more accurately, in order that the activity which has been interrupted by the conflict may go on" (ibid.) She protests that this is not satisfactory because no one wants to give up something. There is also the complication that the contending parties learn to play the game, demanding at the beginning much more than they hope to get, allowing room for cutting down through compromise. In the course of this process, neither side is apt to find out what the other really wants.

Integration is the goal warmly supported by Miss Follett. Neither side gives up anything essential to it and a new amalgam is created into which both positions fit and are respected. To attain this result, thinking must go beyond the original boundaries and creative inventiveness is required. Different from domination and compromise, integration means that the conflict is resolved. She adds that other conflicts will arise but they are apt to be on a higher level, leading to "invention, to the emergence of new values."

81

Miss Follett goes on to suggest some steps in the achievement of integration. One is "to bring the differences out into the open, facing the issues."* This should lead to revaluation, a new examination on the part of each of the contestants of his own position. He may then realize that what he now wants is not quite what he asked for originally. A helpful step is to break down the demands of both sides into their constituent parts, finding "the significant rather than the dramatic features."

Miss Follett recognizes that not all conflicts lend themselves to integration and she outlines specific obstacles to its attainment. Nevertheless she is committed to integration as the best way to deal with conflicts whenever it can be achieved. There is an assumption here about the nature of man and society which would not be shared by thoroughgoing Marxists and Freudians. This aside, Miss Follett's position, with its safeguarding qualifications, has much appeal. It is highly consistent with social work values in which the adjustment and growth of each of the parties is primary. If both get satisfaction and develop through the experience, this is an ideal solution.

Closer to home (group work) is the treatment of conflict in *Social Group Work Practice,* by Gertrude Wilson and Gladys Ryland. Here too we find this subject dignified with importance. For example, "Conflicts and their solutions become the central core of any activity of any group operating in any media of human interest." (p. 52).

The patterns or goals of conflict resolution are based on those presented by Eubank in *The Concepts of Sociology.* They are as follows:

(1) Elimination. They may combat each other, each seeking to win, and if necessary, rid the group of the opposing faction or individual.
(2) Subjugation. The strongest subgroup or individual may force others to accept its point of view and thus dominate the opposition.
(3) Compromise. If the strength of the competing subgroups or individuals is approximately equal, each may give up something to safeguard the activity or the life of the group.
(4) Alliance. Subgroups or individuals may maintain their independence, but combine to achieve a common goal.

---

*Miss Follett does not deal with the possible benefits from deliberate ambiguity when the uncovering and defining of the issues would lead to an impasse.

(5) Integration.   The group as a whole may arrive at a solution that
                    not only satisfies each member but is better than
                    any of the contending suggestions. (p. 53)

Wilson and Ryland clearly favor integration as "the highest of achievement in group life", agreeing with and quoting Follett. They are more specific about patterns of resolution and, of course, relate their material to group work.[3]

Another framework can be added to Follett's and Wilson and Ryland's, one that focuses more on how the conflict is handled by the contestants than on its outcome. It can be thought of as a series of levels, sharing with those cited above built in values which make roughly a desired progression, starting with the lowest level:

1. Physical violence — the attempt to beat the opponent into submission. This behavior is common among children and is of great concern with street gangs. It presents obvious problems. The worker does not want anyone to get hurt. The merits of the two positions receive little attention and the outcome is determined by who is the best fighter. It tends to leave an aftermath of bad feeling and therefore blocks learning how to deal with conflict more maturely. Generally, it belittles and even destroys rationality. The desire for retaliation, as in gang rumbles,[4] has little to do with the reasonableness of the case or even with the truth about what precipitated the fracas in the first place.

2. Verbal violence — the attempt to belittle the opponent, to make him look ridiculous, and to marshal the feelings of the group and others against him. Here, too, the contest is a narrow clash between egos, with alternatives weak or absent in terms of a way of approaching the conflict so that something other than sheer victory or defeat can result.

It is interesting that many street gangs place high value on this verbal combat, sometimes calling it "ranking". The latter term suggests that each party wants to get himself ranked far above the other.

---

[3] An approach which is rooted largely in the field of education is presented in Chapter II of *The Improvement of Practical Intelligence*, by Raup, Axtelle, Benne and Smither, Harper and Brothers, New York, 1950.
[4] For an elaboration of this point about gangs, see Bernstein, Saul, *Youth on the Streets*, Association Press, New York, 1964, p. 55.

While it seems legitimate to place verbal violence a step above physical, the former has roughly similar limitations to the latter, as cited above. The intervention problem of the worker does not seem to be quite as difficult and probably the feelings of the contestants are not so intense. Verbal violence can easily spill over into a physical fight and workers need to be alert to prevent this outcome.

3. Subtler verbal contention — the attempt to belittle and undermine the position of the opponent without violently attacking it. It often involves cleverly citing associated or even irrelevant factors, such as the recalling of an incident in which the antagonist looked foolish or mentioning that anybody who goes to X school must be suspect. There may be a perceptive appraisal of the values, mores and history of the group, leading to a sense of what will work in terms of sarcasm. Guilt by association is a common technique.

While the temperature of this level is not apt to be as high as that of the others, and the worker is likely to find it less difficult to intervene, this level still lacks rationality and is a contest of wit and cleverness rather than a genuine attempt to deal with the issues. The learning by the contesting parties and the others who may be involved is more likely to take the form of a great desire to increase skills in manipulating people through verbal facility than of sorting out facts and issues with clarity.

4. Finding allies — the attempt to line up others to support one's position, which tends to be a power play. Various motives can be presented to potential allies but the main point is to marshal strength which is greater than that of one's opponent. There is the risk that allies will set conditions for their support and then the original protagonist may have to assess whether coming out on top in the conflict is more important to him than are whatever new obligations he accepts from allies. There is also the possibility that the straight edge of the original conflict will be dulled and re-defined by these new conditions and that greater perspective will emerge. Hence the raw ego v. ego quality of the previous stages may take on new and more encouraging dimensions, but this is not always characteristic of the process of enlisting allies.

This level may be combined with others. As indicated, it has more constructive potentialities, it takes time and therefore can allow fierce emotions to diminish. However, it still does not focus primarily on the merits of the issues.

5. Seeking an authoritative decision — the attempt to find someone, probably the group worker, who will say definitively who is wrong and who is right. This is somewhat common in the experience of group workers, especially with children, and the involvement of the worker tends to include factors which extend beyond the conflict. The underlying questions, for example, may be: "Do you like him better than you like me? Did you really mean what you said about being interested in me?" This is the test.

There is the advantage in this level of a search for a resolution which goes beyond a battle of egos. For the worker, it presents many complications and pitfalls but it does make him a meaningful part of the situation and opens opportunities for pursuing new ways of helping the group to think about the conflict. The learning possibilities may be great.

A significant point on this and perhaps other levels stems from the content of the conflict. If facts are at issue, they may not be meaningfully discussable. In a baseball game, for example, whether the runner is out or safe at first base can be argued, but all one can intelligently say is that as I saw it he was out (or safe). Anything further is apt to be derogatory decoration. The worker would be looking for trouble if he as umpire asked what each thought and solicited group discussion. If facts are not known to those involved, the worker should stimulate or undertake himself a search for them. In matters that are primarily opinion, the implications would be quite different.

Recognizing that looking for an arbitrator seems to be steps up from the previous levels, it has a special kind of danger if not handled well. The protagonists could learn to depend on someone else for settling their controversies, thereby losing the opportunity to develop the attitudes and skills which are needed for handling conflict maturely.

6. Creating diversions and delay — the attempt to displace attention on something other than the conflict. Where this level should be placed in the hierarchy is not altogether clear and should depend somewhat on the motivation for creating the diversion. If the mood is such that continuing the discussion at this time would only produce further heat and no light, a diversion would be constructive, although there often is an advantage in sharing with all concerned what the purpose is. Otherwise, there is an element of

manipulation and even trickery. If, on the other hand, the motive is simply to delay action until one party can organize his forces or outwit the other, or if it is to avoid an issue which should be faced, the rating of this method goes down.

There are many occasions when diversion could be helpful and would merit encouragement by the worker. This is especially true when place, time, who is present and the occasion make it difficult to tackle the conflict thoughtfully. Something should be said about picking up on it when circumstances are favorable if the worker thinks the conflict is on-going. It may be wise, rather than creating diversion, to suggest that all had better sleep on it and to offer some thoughts about how the problem might be considered.

7. Respect for differences — a desire to understand how the opponent sees the situation, to collect and head the needed facts, and to attempt to think rationally about the conflict. In no sense does this position or level presuppose or imply a "mush of concession", or taking lightly or apologetically the convictions of either party by themselves or others. False agreements are usually worse than none.

This level, the highest in the hierarchy, has crucial requirements. It is not the first flush of attack and counterattack but rather assumes that a position needs examination and that it may call for modification in the light of factors not previously considered. The willingness to go beyond the clash of egos and the desire to win — deep-rooted as they are — is essential to becoming interested in facts, drawing reasonable conclusions from them and listening carefully to one's opponents.

This approach is not tied or limited to any specific outcome. It could lead to withdrawal (many thoughtful people have resigned from groups because of a basic clash in values), to compromise or to integration. The problem of trying to extend the pie will be considered later but for present purposes the main point is a method which contains the hope of a reasonable resolution.

An element in this level of approach is the readiness to sort out the communal values from those which are at stake in the conflict, and the attempt to weight each. If maintaining the group is regarded as most important, there is then strong leverage for finding a way out of the conflict dilemma. If, on the other hand, the issue is in the realm of the basic values of the group, the question must be faced as to whether it can be maintained without violating something which is just as important or more so.

86

A great advantage in this level is that it is not only hopeful in terms of the immediate conflict but also holds promise for significant learning about dealing with conflict. Group work's concern about the internalizing in the members of new and more desirable values has full application here. Ten years from now, it will probably matter little how the specific conflict comes out, but the increased capacity to handle conflict more maturely matters very much indeed.

A further comment should be made about the dimension of conflict involving its content, which has implications for maturity. Petty personal issues are at one end and subjects of major value concerns at the other. Among children, for example, it is common to have conflicts about turns in a game, name calling and the like. We are troubled when adults indulge in such conflicts expecting them to raise their sights.

Specific Methods of Conflict Resolution

The whole range and dimensions of diagnosis and action in group work should be kept in mind as one considers specific methods dealing with conflict. Whatever may be occurring in groups, our understanding of them collectively and of their individual members is essential to effectiveness, as are our skills in the various facets of intervention. It would be obviously inappropriate in this article to attempt to recapitulate these understandings and skills. They are largely available in the literature. The focus here will rather be on the specifics of methods of dealing with conflict.

A. *Diagnostic* Considerations*

A basic step, although circumstances do not always permit it to come first, is the understanding and assessment of the situation.

---

*As with so many terms in social work, diagnosis presents complications. To some, it may seem too medical, too suggestive of precisely defined categories, especially of pathology. In recent years, however, there has been a trend to use the term in various human relations fields and not to limit it to pathological conditions. For example, "educational diagnosis" has been used in schools of social work to apply to students. Diagnosis can be precise but it need not be so. Essentially, it involves stocktaking or assessment in the framework of whatever variables are regarded as important with whatever information is available in relation to the variables. Diagnosis implies the importance of understanding a situation in order to act intelligently on it.

Does a conflict, as characterized above, actually exist? What is scarce? Who are contending? How did it develop? Is the issue real or unreal? Are communal values at a stake? These and other broad questions, if well answered, can lead to a helpful orientation. But let's be more specific.

How strong and even uncontrolled are the feelings of the contenders? Is the history of the group full of sudden flare-ups, uncontrolled impulses, which come and go without continuing clashes between the same two parties, or is this a long-standing difficulty? What might be the cumulative effects and retaliatory efforts if the conflict is allowed full expression? In casework, a client can express his side of the story to the worker without the opponent knowing it and responding. In this sense, strong feelings are safer to get out than is true in groups, where the interplay may rise in intensity and rush out of control. This element of the strength of the feeling is a central clue as to whether to encourage or permit the group process to go its way, or to divert it or postpone it, or to help to establish firm ground rules to control the expression of feeling. The worker should also be sensitive to what may happen later, when he is not present and should try to leave the situation in a state where communication between the opponents is no longer violent. If the conflict is not within the group but between it and another group, or it is directed against the agency or the worker, much of the spirit of the above would apply, except that one would hope that strong feelings on the part of the group could be accepted by staff members without retaliation and that the process of resolution can be started by the worker's ability to show that this kind of feeling can be understood by professionals, even though they do not accept the content of what is said.

The time factor has been referred to in terms of the duration of the conflict. There is also the immediate time dimension. If something else is scheduled soon, it would be best to try to get a postponement. It would be unfortunate if the consideration of the problem had to be stopped in its early stages or when only one party has had the opportunity to state its case. A general understanding could be reached to delay the discussion until an appropriate time or to cancel the interrupting event.

The alignment of personalities, subgroups and indigenous leadership is apt to be revealing. We may frequently find for example, that A supports B because A feels very inadequate and he finds in *B* the strength he yearns for in himself. Or *A* supports *B* out of hostility to the latter's opponent, *C.* Or something about *C* touches off in *A* mechanisms arising in his own sibling situations. Of a somewhat different order is some plus group affiliation with *B*, such as religion, class, school, both being charter members, and the like. Of a still different order is a thoughtfully held position on the issue, without undue regard for who happens to be on which side.

A potent dimension is whether the alignment of opponents has quite a history and pertains to practically all decisions and conflicts. A proposition — not mentioned in Coser's book — suggests that this type of conflict is severe and consuming. Its existence calls for a careful examination of whether the communal values have any great significance. Certainly, one ought not to let such a situation slide along.

In contrast is the more limited kind of conflict where the alignment applies to the immediate issue, with some opponents joining forces on other questions against some of those with whom they had agreed. This provides for some watering down of the intensity of feeling and the probable lessening of its duration. One is apt to be more careful about what is said to an opponent with whom one agrees on other matters and whose support will be needed. This may or may not be a conscious process.

The personality dynamics of the contestants help the worker to understand the conflict and to intervene constructively. As an illustration, free floating hostility, going back into the family history of the member, may happen to descend on particular issues and members. The implication would be to try to deal with the feelings in a variety of ways rather than to set up a careful and long-range plan to tackle the issues.

In a street gang of older adolescents, the worker had established a relationship with them a few months ago. After various complications, officers had been elected and some new program activities were beginning to develop. In not too long, feeling began to mount against the officers. The specific grievances were not too clear, taking largely the form of complaints about domination by what was regarded as a clique. The tension rose to the point where the worker saw no alternative to an emotionally charged session in which the feelings would be fully expressed. It was indeed a violent session, with heated accusations and defences and counteraccusations. It ended with the decision to have a new election and, interestingly enough, all the officers were re-elected!

Various interpretations can be made of this strange sequence. The problem of coming to grips with authority was acute with these boys. Many kinds of authority had been the object of hostility and rebellion. The kind they might accept, from within the gang has now been invaded and modified by the efforts of the worker to introduce more democratic processes, making it safer to challenge the elected leaders. The psychological elements arising in their families and sub-culture motivated them to fight, in a mixed way, any kind of authority. These feelings had to come out and yet there probably was guilt about expressing them. Hence the re-election of the same boys was a neat solution and the whole experience seems to have been cathartic and maturing. This is an excellent illustration of a conflict in which the ostensible issues around the behavior of the officers were merely pegs on which to hang important feelings arising from personality and sub-culture dynamics. To understand this is to free the worker to deal more effectively with the conflict. There are many variations in the patterns of specific situations, but the general point holds that awareness of personality and cultural dynamics illuminates the conflict, especially when solid issues are not present. Displacement and scapegoating are particularly to be watched.

Just as people are influenced by forces which are intrapsychic and in the immediate group, they are also very much affected by other or reference groups. In a given conflict, a protagonist may be as much moved by people not present as he is by those he faces. The representative kind of group is an obvious example. A representative in it may think that what his opponent is saying makes sense but that he would be a traitor to the group he represents if he admitted it and could be quoted back home to that effect. He feels that he must be able to say later that he put up a great fight.

The reference group idea can be expanded to include not only other well defined small groups of which an individual is a member and to which he feels loyalty and responsibility, but also larger segments of our society which are less clearly defined, such as religion, class, race, neighborhood, a profession, an age level and the like. Whenever a conflict arises in a specific group there is the potential for arousing these outside and larger loyalties with the result that they may well become central, if not always recognized, components of the conflict. The awareness on the part of the worker that these larger social systems are being invoked enables him to understand the conflict more fully.

As has been stated earlier in this article, groups inevitably involve differences of many kinds. In order to function, attitudes toward differences and ways of dealing with them must be developed so that they do not destroy the enterprise or block its development to the extent that little satisfaction is afforded the members. A specialized kind of study and diagnosis could be done along this dimension. Are the boundaries for accepting or working with differences close together and tight, a kind of low difference quotient, with compelling demands for conformity? Is the group quick to want to put out the variant or deviant and to want to crush his dissent? How do these moods get expressed in times of crisis, especially if there is an external threat which usually has the effect of requiring greater unity often seen as rigid conformity?

The content of the differences may be highly significant. For example, in the early days of a settlement house, the two ethnic groups composing most of its membership did not mix in any groups in which the choice of members was open. The staff stimulated the formation of councils, committees and others in which both ethnic groups participated, but friendship groups and most interest groups were of one nationality or the other. Their universe could not comfortably include this kind of difference. Ten years later, ethnic origin was hardly relevant and practically all groups included both ethnic backgrounds and some of other nationalities. This particular boundary had changed markedly in a relatively short time. Other limits, however, did exist. It so happens that Negroes and Jews did not live in this neighborhood. If they had, they would probably have encountered strong boundaries against them in many of the groups. There were limits of other kinds. There was a fringe of anti-social gang activities in this area. Those who had never been in this type of gang or who had moved out of its characteristic behavior were not ready to tolerate current gang members in agency groups and were not wholly sympathetic with the agency's efforts to welcome such gangs as groups in its program. I recall vividly heated arguments between the two points of view. A gang member insisted that it was not safe in this neighborhood to be unaffiliated with a gang, while the others cited their own experience to show that this protection was not needed.

Still another aspect of boundaries can be cited from the same agency. There was a strong anti-school and anti-intellectual tradition among the young people. If any of them read serious books, they would not dare to mention it. The staff used imaginative ways of introducing dramatic material from books, but the going was rough. Here, too, was an element of the boundaries of the acceptance of differences. There seemed to be a recognition that the staff did read and found education meaningful, but these characteristics in members would have been objectionable.

The above are merely illustrations of the kinds of differences which may enter into conflicts. There could be many others. In summary of this dimension of conflict, both the general mood about differences and the attitudes toward specific variances need to be examined to understand and act upon group conflicts.

The decision-making process is central to group life.* Here, too, a specialized study and diagnosis could be made in terms of the tone and the methods in accordance with which groups make decisions. It is inevitable that over a period of time certain procedures will be institutionalized, i.e., taken for granted as ways of making decisions. Drawing lots or tossing a coin is one technique (not a bad one for some situations). Following the dictates of a high status person is another. A thoughtful discussion which examines carefully the relevant factors is still another procedure. There could be a vote or obtaining a general sense of the trend of opinion is still another. (Voting, a heavily used method, is subject to some limitations which should be recognized in group work.) Whatever may be the specific techniques used by the group, the resources within it in terms of more or less established ways of reaching decisions should be an important part of the assessment of the conflict situation by the worker. The problem could be as much or more in the decision-making process as it is in substantive issues. Sometimes the difficulty is that this process has not been clear and one part of the group thinks that a decision has been made while another part does not. New ways of making decisions may be needed.

---

*This point is further developed in the succeeding article in this book.

The position of the worker in relation to the group has potent implications for his opportunity to be active and helpful. If he has not established a meaningful relationship to the group, if some members involved in the conflict are still suspicious of him, he might well move cautiously and even wait to be asked to help, unless behavior is taking extreme forms. If, on the other hand, trust has been developed and members sense his wise use of the professional role, he is freer to intervene.

A final dimension of diagnosis involves an appraisal of the flexible and more rigid components so that the worker can formulate a strategy for change. This includes thinking ahead to attempt to anticipate the consequences of each line of action. Should he, for example, remain quiet and permit the group process to unfold? Are the positions so rigidly and heatedly held that emotions would run wild? Is the main and stable dynamic the struggle for status by the leader of one of the contending parties? If so, are there possibilities for meeting this need without the necessity for defeating his opponent? Is the subject of the contention basic and apparently irreconcilable? Would it then be best to consider splitting the group? These and other questions indicate what is meant here by strategy.

B. *Specific Methods of Dealing with Conflict**

In the foregoing, much has been said directly and indirectly about methods of dealing with conflict. It seems desirable, however, to focus here on what the worker does, which is the bridge between his diagnosis and his goals. Because these aspects of professional practice are set up somewhat separately in this article does not mean, of course, that they occur separately or in some defined succession. Values, goals, diagnosis and action interrelate and interact in actuality. The worker knows some things and makes a diagnosis. He acts on it and watches sensitively for the feedback. He may then revise his diagnosis and try something else, all in relation to values and goals.

A good starting point about methods is that the worker should consistently try to maintain a relationship with the whole group.

---

*To avoid a detour into semantics, the term "specific methods" is used to include functions, methods, techniques and perhaps more. I have in mind the application of skill in patterns of worker activity directed toward the achievement of conscious goals and the implementation of professional values.

One party to the conflict may be the embodiment of reason and justice, with the other quite opposite. Nevertheless, the responsibility of the worker is to all members — a difficult task — and he should not move, or permit himself to be moved, in the direction of supporting one party and rejecting, opposing or abandoning the other. Otherwise, he may find a seemingly sound resolution of the particular situation, without the potential for further work with these abandoned. This is not easy to do without giving the impression that only cordial relations count regardless of the merits of substantive issues. At some point, it may be desirable for the worker to state his own position on the conflict, but he must do so in such a way that those opposed are not alienated.

All this may present his most difficult task to the group worker, but it is not an impossible one. A professional role which combines concern about the people served, honestly held convictions, the use of developed methods, and other components, is not easily achieved, but it does seem to be achievable. My clear impression is that this is what members learn to expect from group workers and what they find most helpful, especially in the differentiation stage as described in the previous article.

There are many pulls which tend to throw this role out of balance. Inevitably some members appeal to the worker more than others. If these favored members are all on one side of a conflict, the worker's professional stance may sway or stray. Or the content of the conflict may touch off such deep feelings and convictions on the part of the worker that this is all he is able to encompass. Especially to be cautioned against is the temptation to think in terms of the vital test being only the unfolding of cordial human relations. This could easily result in the elevation of methods and expectations about resolving conflicts at the cost of evaluating honestly held, rationally and reality based differing convictions. Under such circumstances, maintaining the group as a social system may be difficult and even questionable. The vitally interested concern of the worker in all members would be especially important.

If the conflict is between the group and another party outside it, the worker often faces delicate decisions. He may have various thoughts about how right or wrong his group is, but his responsibility is to stay with the members without necessarily endorsing their point of view. If, as in the movie, "The Boy with the Knife", the group is put out of a playground because of obstreperous

94

behavior, the worker walks out with them. This is just the point at which they need him most. He can help the members to express their strong feelings and, over time, to attain perspective on the relationship between their behavior and its consequences. In various ways, he is helping to create a new model for them of ways to deal with conflict. He does not get into an argument with the playground worker and sets the tone for a reasonable acceptance of authority. He is understanding of the boys' feelings and yet has the opportunity to help them to think about the other side of the picture. All this has a more mature quality than the impulsive and aggressive reactions typical of these boys. Far from the least important consideration is the point that however violent their antagonistic feelings may be at any given time, there is practically always available the potential for a more balanced view if the mood and stimuli are appropriate for reaching and supporting this potential. Even with the toughest street gangs, there are such possibilities as the fear of getting hurt in a rumble, the vague feeling, perhaps deeply buried, that this way of handling conflict does not make sense, and that the other gang may not be quite as bad as it seems.

If the conflict is with another staff member or agency policy, there is the added complication that the worker will be expected by the group to identify to some extent with his colleagues and with the agency which employs him, which is as it should be. Groups can be clever about putting workers in difficult positions. They might say that there is no point in discussing the problem with the worker because he is bound to stand up for his colleagues. Or they may make extreme statements against other workers. These and other forms of baiting may strain the worker's professional stance. If he is highly competitive with the other worker, he may take a snide satisfaction in the criticisms and the members are apt to catch this.

If he is still in the adolescent struggle with authority, he might too obviously enjoy hearing his supervisor getting taken apart. These feelings, while understandable, must be disciplined and outgrown if the worker is to be of significant help to the members. It would be unwise to defend every action of his colleagues or every policy of his agency. Criticisms can be listened to sympathetically, without endorsing them. Ways can be developed for further communication with the other staff members and for obtaining clarifying information. The worker may be able to make explanations of the rationale behind policies which had not occurred to the members.

Conflict between parties of approximately the same strength often calls for a kind of referee role from the worker, the establishment and maintenance of ground rules which insure fair play. When, however, the relative strengths are quite unequal, the worker should try to prevent abuse and exploitation, and to help the weaker party to assert itself and to articulate its case. This often requires appealing in the group or outside of it to the sense of fair play and group loyalty in the stronger party, as it does encouragement and support of the weaker.

There is the gray area where it is not clear whether a conflict exists. A controlling clique may be fully contented with the state of affairs and unaware of the dissatisfaction felt by those controlled. This is far from rare among dominant groups. Or they may realize what they are doing and find it quite zestful. These situations are gray areas in relation to conflict because, although the potentials are there, a direct clash has not occurred. The worker faces the question of whether a clear conflict would be helpful to the group and, if so, should he try to precipitate it.

Several complex dimensions need to be examined. Would the dominant clique respond to an attempt to help them to understand what they are doing and to change? This sometimes works. Can the subjugated be stimulated gradually to assert themselves? This is more likely to lead to conflict. In many situations change in the distribution of power can come only through conflict and the latter may well present more constructive possibilities than would a continuation of the domination pattern.

In moving in this direction, several assessments need to be made. Is the worker's relationship with both parties sufficiently strong that he can help both through the conflict? Is there such a difference in strength that the result is apt to be a reinforcement of the old pattern rather than the evolution of a new one? Can the worker proceed in a way that either or both parties will not feel manipulated by his techniques, but will understand that his concern has the integrity of trying honestly and maturely to help with the solution of problems firmly embedded in the realities of the group?

A particularly difficult factor to anticipate is whether the free expression of antagonistic feelings will run wild and be highly damaging. In one instance, two clubs had been developing a feud for some time. A staff member, who knew and was trusted by both groups, had talked separately with each of them, and he decided to call them together. He took vigorous leadership, saying that something had to be done and frankly shared his concern that a discussion of this kind could easily get out of control. Therefore, he would insist that no one speak without first being recognized by him. The feeling about the staff member was sufficiently positive that these older adolescents accepted this framework and seemed almost relieved to have it. There were times when the rule was broken, but he quickly intervened and reminded them of it. All points of view were heard and since objective issues were not very much involved, the expression of feelings seemed to clear the air and the conflict died down. There are other occasions when the less disciplined expression of feelings might work well. The danger to be watched for by the worker is the cumulative effect of accusation and counter-accusation so that the conflict takes on more difficult dimensions through the effort to resolve it. This kind of anticipation is not easy.

In situations involving agency policy, there may be a question of which staff member should deal with the conflict. In a settlement house some years ago there was a plan whereby older adolescents and young adults who showed leadership potential and did volunteer work were given exclusive use of a room and some other privileges. At one time the plan degenerated into great concern for the privileges and an unwillingness to undertake responsibilities. Various approaches were tried and failed. The staff decided then to withdraw the privileges with the hope that responsibilities could gradually be developed. Since this decision was reached in the late Spring, and a new student worker would be arriving in the Fall, I as a member of the ongoing staff was asked to break the news to the boys and to work on the situation with them over the Summer. It was highly unpleasant and my status with these boys went way down. Nevertheless, it would have been loading too much on the new student worker to ask him to announce this explosive decision as his first contact with the group.

It has sometimes been suggested that this kind of separation between the "good" worker and the "bad father" or disciplinarian (another staff member usually on a higher administrative level) should be maintained generally, especially with aggressive groups. This is artificial and would tend to reinforce immature ways of dealing with conflict in relation to authority, particularly the assumption that the whole problem is in the "they" up above with no need for the group to work on its own contribution toward it and a way of communicating with and working out a better adjustment to authority. The difficulty may not be entirely in the group and each agency needs to review thoughtfully its policies and procedures which precipitate conflicts with members. Nevertheless, the group's worker is also an agency representative and he helps best by acting on the variety of roles built into his function, rather than just selecting the pleasant ones. Being close to the group, he is in the best position to help with conflict.

An interesting dichotomy often develops when group workers go into hospitals, particularly where children are the patients. Doctors, nurses, physical therapists and perhaps others frequently offer treatment which is painful, tedious or irritating. The group worker, on the other hand, is apt to provide very pleasant experiences. This is a circumstantial advantage which should be used to support the other services. A child may need to express his fears about surgery, he may need a fuller interpretation of why the nurses insist on certain routines, and the like. The group worker should share responsibly in the necessary authority patterns in the institution.

The practice of working individually and with sub-units in group work has potentials for dealing with conflict. Away from the opposing party, the worker can encourage the fuller expression of feeling without the worry of retaliation. The more extreme forms of aggression may be thus drained off before the opponent is confronted. After this stage, the worker can raise questions and point out things which lead to greater perspective. He can try to protect the person or sub-group from the consequences of the heated expression of violent feelings under conditions which would produce strong responses. He can also help to relate this situation to others in a way to move toward greater self-awareness on the part of the member(s).

Reference groups, as suggested above, are frequently important dimensions of conflict. One or more members feels that regardless of what anyone present may say, he has a fixed obligation to another group to maintain a given position. In this context, the position may not be intelligently discussable and the protagonist may not even share with the group his central motivation for fighting so hard on the specific issue. It is helpful to all concerned to have this loyalty frankly expressed.

98

An interesting illustration of how a reference group enters into a conflict occurred a few years ago in a Jewish Center. A council composed of representatives from teenage clubs was planning a picnic for their groups as the culmination of an active season. The date, place and other details were fixed and the affair was warmly anticipated. Then a bombshell dropped in the form of an announcement from the AZA club (a part of the national B'nai B'rith program) that a baseball game was scheduled for that day with another AZA club. To hold the picnic without this group would have deprived it of some of the most active and appealing boys. Ideas were tried out by way of combining the picnic and the baseball game (Follett's integration?) but practical difficulties made that impossible. The worker was quite concerned and very critical of AZA. At someone's suggestion, he called the AZA regional office and found that they did not know of the conflict. They were glad to change the date of the ball game and all concerned were pleased. This incident illustrates the danger that the perception that a member of one group has of his obligation to another may not be accurate or immovable. The AZA boys just assumed that if the game was scheduled it had to take place at that time and place. It never occurred to them that the date could be changed.

If the member's perception of his obligation to the reference group is correct, the assessment shifts. The problem then becomes one of reconciling somehow a position taken outside the group with an opposing one strongly held within the group. The nature of the outside position and the loyalty to it call for examination. Is the reference group reachable by someone? Are its members aware of the conflict and have they thought of what it involves? If the reference group is a religion or a social class, how firmly rooted in it is the member? In his values, how do the two groups rank? Is he in the process of moving into or away from either group? Do the opposing members understand the strength of the pull of the reference group on their fellow member? Then there is the area of weighing the specific issues and of attempting various approaches, but this will be dealt with below. The function of the worker in relation to reference groups is to help the members clarify these questions and to understand that all of us have multiple group loyalties which tend to influence us, and that such loyalties command respect.

Not exclusively on the matter of reference groups is the

concept of a larger or new social system entering into the conflict in a way to give it new dimensions. The worker, as one example, might suggest that other groups have encountered this kind of conflict and that it might be interesting to find out how they handled it. As another approach, it is reasonably common to have inter-agency conferences on a local, regional or national level. There are still other possibilities.

An additional approach is to change the composition of the group. In a newly formed club of elderly members, there was a preoccupation with playing cards to the exclusion of other activities. This was in conflict with the agency's aim for the group. The worker's attempts to stimulate new activities failed and it was suggested to her that she recruit new members on the assumption that they would probably have different interests. This turned out to be true. In another situation, the group was formed to help a girl with certain problems. Unfortunately, the recruited members did not like her and were punishing toward her, conflicting with the agency's purpose in forming the group. The staff decided to introduce some new girls into the group, hoping that they would serve as a bridge. There was strong opposition from all except the original girl for whom the group was formed. After a time, the picture changed and the purpose of the staff in bringing in the new girls was largely realized. The skill and emotional poise of the worker were important elements in the change.

To pull things together, an existing group experiencing conflict does not in itself exhaust the relevant dimensions. Reference groups play their part. It may be possible to throw the conflict on to a larger canvas. It may also be feasible and desirable to change the composition of the group. These are factors and resources available to the worker.

The specific methods of dealing with the issues in the conflict command attention. In some instances, the problem may have arisen from an inaccurate rumor. In a loosely organized street gang, a girl lined up quite an army to fight another girl because of something the latter was supposed to have said. The worker carefully checked the facts and was convinced that this remark had never been made, at least in the form in which it reached its subject. The worker discussed this point carefully alone with each of the two girls and then brought them together. Both were glad to make peace. Conflict lends itself so easily to rumor and distortion, especially with those whose emotions are volatile, that this sober fact finding and sifting out process, involving the contestants at appropriate points, may be all that is needed in some instances.

Perhaps the greatest contribution the worker can make is to help to sort out the issues and to clarify areas of agreement and disagreement. There is the temptation to exaggerate the former and to shrink the latter, but this will not be helpful in the long run because disregarded or belittled issues in conflicts have a way of popping up again. The worker must be careful not to solve the problem for the group, but he can raise questions which stimulate the members to think of approaches, such as compromise, arbitration and integration. He may find it desirable to urge postponement of a decision so that more thought can be devoted to it. With his better eye on what members are learning, and a good eye on how the specific conflict is being handled, he would do well at an appropriate point to encourage an evaluation of how the conflict has been handled, perhaps making comparisons with such episodes in the past. The articulation of learning can serve to solidify it.

One of the major general roles of the worker is that of a resource in terms of activities, places to go, services available, and ways of dealing with relationship problems. This role has rich meaning in terms of conflict. Members should not feel that they are alone in a jungle of raw and uncomfortable emotion. There are things that can be done about such unpleasant situations and the worker provides this structure insofar as the members are not able to do so.

An intriguing opportunity for the worker arises from the core of the concept of conflict, i.e., something (values, position, possessions, etc.) is scarce; there is not enough to go around and what one party gains the other loses. The pie is perceived as having fixed dimensions. Whether this is actually true in any specific conflict needs exploration. Recognizing that we are not always able to extend the pie so that each of the contenders receives a reasonable share, we should not begin by assuming that its size and value are fixed. Perhaps some illustrations will help.

Two members are fighting hard for the presidency of the group. Both want it very much and each has lined up supporters. As these two see the situation, there is only one desired office and only one of them can win it. The pie is clear and scarce. The vice-presidency or some other office would not satisfy.

A group of boys in their late teens — this is an actual case — had a long and rich history as a club, and they wanted very much to continue. However, about half of them had moved away. Those remaining decided to invite new members to join, and this was done. The old members regarded the new ones largely as a means for continuing their club. The late comers, on the other hand, saw the situation as a new club, and — this really hurt — calling for a new name. The conflict raged and unfortunately the boys did not have a worker.

A group of boys had been friends for a long time. Now their interests were diverging. Some played on the club team in a league; the rest did not have the ability or were not interested. Somehow this situation was handled without severe strain until one of the athletes suggested using the club treasury to buy basketball uniforms. This precipitated a full-blown conflict.

Illustrations could be further multiplied, but the point is to show various kinds of scarcity and pies. As to whether any of the above pies could have been extended so that both parties would have been satisfied is hard to know, but there are situations in which something approaching the increase of the scarce item can be achieved.

Indigenous leadership is often regarded by members of groups as scarce and as a source of conflict, i.e., there can be only one leader. We are now thinking of leadership in terms of a series of functions which can be, and often are, distributed among two or more members. At a given time, there may be the question of who is to be elected president, who is to be captain of the team, or of who is to occupy whatever position may carry the highest status. The concern could be about a leadership position which is not formalized in any designated office, but it involves informal leadership with its large component of being able to influence others. At the moment of the conflict the minds and feelings of the members may be so set in the framework of a one leader pattern that it is not possible then to extend the pie. As time moves along, however, and activities and situations change, new areas for leadership can be opened and other individuals may well fill them. There will still be some element of scarcity about leadership, but the heat tends to be dispersed over a larger territory, with the hope that conflict will be less intense. It is an important aim of the group worker to encourage this diversity of

102

leaders and, more generally, to increase the role repertoire and diversity in the group.

A comparable line of reasoning can be followed whether the subject is the selection of activities, the use of the treasury, the admission of new members, or other matters. It may happen that with the best thinking and imagination on the part of the group and the worker, the pie is still as small as ever, but, with a long view and a vigorous search, ways can sometimes be found to stretch the pie. Members might have ideas about this and the worker should encourage their expression as well as contribute his own thoughts.

This leads into another method and function of the worker, requiring some explanation. A conflict can be symbolically represented by $A \leftrightarrow B$, with A and B representing the contending parties (not necessarily individuals). If the conflict is severe and the stakes are great, both A and B may become so preoccupied with winning that they lose sight of greater values which they have in common, of what their struggle may do to the group and to themselves, of whether their methods of fighting each other are within the realm of reason and acceptability, and even of what they are fighting about. This picture is presented somewhat extremely to clarify the meaning of concern only about being victorious in a conflict.

For a helpful resolution, there is needed another kind of role which does not lose sight of the factors mentioned in the preceding paragraph. This role could be present in members of the group not immediately involved in the conflict, in the president who is presumed to have some of this quality built into his functions, and even in one or both protagonists. It certainly should be in the worker both in terms of understanding and action. In relation to the members, it would be unfortunate to identify this perspective role entirely with any one person. It could shift from time to time and the aim of the worker is to stimulate its widest possible spread among the members.

Perhaps the perspective role should be elaborated. Its complete opposite makes winning the conflict, beating the opponent, the king value. Perspective begins with such thoughts as whether innocent bystanders may be hurt, the group could be wrecked, the victory may not be quite what it was previously thought to be, status and friends may be lost, and many other possibilities. By and large, these factors apply to the way the conflict is approached more than they do to its content. Perspective has implications for

103

the intensity of feeling but it should not be regarded as anti-conviction. The party to the conflict who goes through the suggested processes may still come out even more firmly devoted to the original position, and this is to be respected. Perspective should not lead to mushiness. Rather it should evoke a larger framework which relates the conflict to relevant people, situations and values.

As with various constructive roles which enter into the worker's image of a mature group, he might well wait for this perspective one to be taken by one or more members. If it appears indigenously, he then should support and amplify it, trying to have the whole group recognize its merits. If no member expresses this mood, the worker has the responsibility for doing so. There are many difficult questions of timing, etc., but this general recognition of roles in relation to conflict can provide basic guidelines. Furthermore, it has roots in strong desires, on the surface or buried under hostilities, to find some way out of a painful situation. Keeping in mind the professional goal of helping members to learn how to handle conflict maturely as being more important than any specific resolution, the establishment and building firmly into the group the perspective role assumes central significance. Another way of saying this is that over the long pull the worker should operate in such a way as to make himself decreasingly needed. The developing ability of members of the group to incorporate into themselves this perspective role in conflict is one of the more crucial tests of how far he has moved toward his professionally sound exit from the group.

Concluding Comments

Conflicts involving groups can be between individuals, sub-groups, one member and all the others, the group and another group, the group and the worker, the group and the agency, etc. While each of these situations may have distinctive characteristics, this article would have become labored and overburdened if every kind of party alignment had been discussed in relation to each aspect of conflict. It seemed best to focus mostly on intra-group conflict with some attention to other kinds. It is hoped that the ideas presented will have broad application.

The opportunities for the group worker to influence the handling of conflict vary considerably. Again it did not seem desirable to go into the complexities of this factor at multiple points. The stance was taken that if the worker could effectively intervene, what should be the nature and direction of his activity?

Important as it is, conflict is only one dimension of group processes. Social work and group work are committed to the constellation approach, i.e., to giving full heed to all factors which are regarded as relevant. Hence the focus on conflict may legitimately give the impression of being segmented or partial. It is hoped that the reader will react in this way. Nevertheless, for orderly thinking and to move toward new understanding and methods, there are great advantages in this kind of abstraction. The various and multitudinous specifics of any given group were not included, but a frame of reference for understanding and dealing with conflict is helpful in working on the specifics of any one group.

As a final point, it is well to come back to the concept of conflict as pervasive and normal and as an opportunity for growth. In the course of dealing with it, members of groups can be helped to see problems and situations in new ways, to call on strengths within themselves which had been dormant, and to develop a set of attitudes and skills which will make a tremendous contribution to their future functioning as mature people. Only as the worker grasps these vivid and vast potentialities can he help the group to realize them.

REFERENCES

BERNSTEIN, SAUL, "Charting Group Progress", in *Readings in Group Work*, Dorothea Sullivan, ed., Association Press New York, 1952.
– – – – – – – – – *Youth on the Streets*, Association Press, New Hork, 1964.
COSER, LEWIS, *The Functions of Group Conflict*, Free Press, Glencoe, Illinois, 1956.
FOLLETT, MARY P., *Dynamic Administration*, collected papers, edited by Metcalf and Urwick, Harper and Brothers, New York and London, 1940.
GARLAND, JAMES A., JONES, HUBERT E., and KOLODNY, RALPH L., *A Model for Stages of Development in Social Group Work*, see preceding article in this book.
LOWY, LOUIS, *Decision-Making and Group Work*, see succeeding article in this book.
MACK and SNYDER, "The Analysis of Social Conflict", Free Press, Glencoe, Illinois, 1956.

PUMPHREY, MURIEL, "The Teaching of Values and Ethics in Social Work Education", Vol. XIII, Curriculum Study, Council on Social Work Education, 1959.

RAUP, AXTELLE, BENNE and SMITHER, "The Improvement of Practical Intelligence", Harper and Brothers, New York, 1950.

WILSON, GERTRUDE and RYLAND, GLADYS, *Social Group Work Practice,* Houghton Mifflin, Co., Boston, 1959.

Chapter 4

DECISION-MAKING AND GROUP WORK

Louis Lowy

Group theorists recognize that decision-making is inherent in the group process, and group workers have always held that the decision-making process should be utilized in the fulfilment of group-work objectives. In fact, Wilson and Ryland (1950) state it quite clearly:

> Since the decision-making process is the central core of the social group work method, it is essential that the structure be such that the members have the privileges and responsibilities of the management of their own corporate affairs. A collection of individuals will not develop the characteristics of a social group unless they have the right and the ability to make decisions significant to their own group life. Nor will they grow and develop unless they experience the difficulty which comes from the adjustment of personal claims to the claims of the group as a whole. (p. 66).

Although there has been an increasing interest in decision-making, the scientific study of it is still in an early stage of development. As Wasserman and Silander put it succinctly: "The literature's sum-total is to be found in a widely scattered group of writings which cut across all areas of social and scientific inquiry."[1]

---

[1] Wasserman, P. & Silander, Fred. *Decision-Making,* an Annotated Bibliography, Graduate School of Business in Public Administration, Cornell University, Ithaca, New York, 1958, p. iv.

Decision-making takes place in a variety of contexts. It occurs on the part of individuals and in social situations which increase the complexity of dealing with it. It takes place among the smallest unit of social interaction, i.e., two people; it occurs among small groups, larger groupings, formal organizations such as bureaucracies, on the community level whether in the neighborhood or the country, the state, and national level and in the international arena. The components of the collective system and its size have a bearing upon the nature of decision-making and are therefore important variables in the process itself.

Since our concern here is with the decision-making process in group work, we want to look at its nature in small groups and then to review decision-making within the context of group work.

Nature of the Decision-making Process and Small Groups

Every person in his life is faced with making choices presumed to be based on the availability of alternatives. To make a choice essentially means to select from available alternatives and to implement this selection. In some situations, there are numerous alternatives available, which may not be cognitively known to the central person. Therefore, we can say that the "real" alternatives available are only those that are within a perceptual, cognitive field of a particular person; they are based on his background, characteristics of personality, and the social and cultural experiences which have shaped his personality, and upon which he can draw to make choices. It is often assumed that decision-making ought to be a rational process, attempting to reduce non-rational as well as irrational factors. We know, however, that this value assumption is not based in fact; unconscious factors are powerful forces in restricting people from making the choices that are conceived to be in the rational self-interest. Besides, we can differentiate between those decisions which are within the control of individuals and groups and those which are presently beyond their control. Examples of the latter are such natural phenomena as weather conditions, cataclysmic events, etc. Throughout history man has continuously strived to subjugate natural forces and social events to his power and control and to increase the degree and frequence of controlling the decision-making process. But recognition of the limitations of decision-control is an essential element, if we are concerned with helping people to understand the decision-making process and to assist them in becoming more adept and rational in arriving at decisions.

Decisions lead to consequences. The conscious decision-process is based on premises and, depending upon the nature of these premises, the consequences of the decision will be felt. During the process of decision-making only some of these consequences can be anticipated because many of them are not within the purview of the participants at that time.

To achieve collective action, group members must participate in decision-making processes in group life. These processes disclose the personally held values of individual members and indicate potential conflicts. Through interpersonal relationships, group members will make alignments and alliances, subgroups will shift in response to various types of accommodations and solutions. "In every group, sooner or later, a decision-making apparatus must be agreed upon. Whether it be consensus, majority rule, unanimity or any other method, there must be some *modus operandi* for the group to make decisions.' (Schutz (1962) p. 298).

Every group will develop a method to "get things done", to achieve its general goals and its specific objectives. Out of this desire emerges a group structure which differentiates the members according to their functional roles, which, in Bales's (1950) view is essential to achieve "a system of solutions . . . in order to reduce the tensions growing out of uncertainty and unpredictability in the actions of others". (p. 80). Or, as Schutz phrases it: "People have a need to maintain a satisfactory relation between oneself and other people with regard to power and influence. In other words, every individual has a need to control his situation to some degree, so that his environment can be predictable for him." (op. cit., p. 298).

Controlling needs are reciprocal. People want to control and be controlled. They vary, however, on the degree of each. At one end of this continuum, there are people who want to control everyone (e.g., dominate the entire group); on the other, there are people who do not want to control anyone in particular. There are people who want to be completely controlled by others (they are dependent on others for making decisions for them) and those who want to be controlled under no conditions (they are the ones who want to make all the decisions).

As can be seen from these statements, decision-making processes are linked with control, influence, authority, and therefore they are related to group structures. To be involved in decision-making is not only a fundamental condition of group life, but is also essential for the individual member in relation to his own needs relative to control and authority.

The literature on decision-making in small groups is primarily concerned with "task-oriented groups", and only to a lesser degree with "growth-oriented" (developmental) groups. Productivity of group effort, power relationships, group pressures on individual judgment, and group effectiveness are some of the most frequently investigated aspects of decision making. Wasserman and Silander (op. cit.) in their annotated bibliography on decision-making, devote a chapter to "Decision-making in small groups" in which they cite many studies in the literature mostly developed by social-psychologists. Hare (1962), in *Handbook of Small Group Research,* emphasizes mostly the relationship between decision-making, inter-action, and perception.

In reviewing these studies, one is again struck by the inter-relationships of many group variables and their impact upon decision-making. There is virtually nothing that occurs in the life of a small group which does not have bearing upon decision-making and vice versa. The author's verdict in their introduction that ". . . attempts to synthesize (the literature) have been isolated and uncommon" (op. cit.), is one of the major obstacles to the develop-ment of a coherent theory.

Much of the reported research on decision making has been conducted in the laboratory and relatively few studies have been made among "group-in-the-raw". Group work, while focusing on both task and growth-oriented (developmental) groups, has been mostly concerned with the latter type, since group work as one of the helping methods of social work is oriented and geared to the development and nurturing aspects of group relationships for individual members.

Decision-Making and Group Work

In any type of group, decisions are made and a mechanism for this process will develop sooner or later. Because of the nature and purpose of group work, the decision-making process takes on characteristics which are different from the comparable process in other types of group endeavors. In a "group work" group, the function of the decision-making process is to utilize it primarily for

110

the benefit of the group members. Individuals should be helped to come to terms with their needs for the achievement for power, controls, and with their feelings regarding authority. The group-as-a-whole is perceived as an instrumentality to meet these among other needs. It is also an instrumentality to help members experience the nature of making choices, of subordinating their wishes and desires for the greater good, and for transferring the new behavior to other situations. When a member has learned in one group how to cope with alternatives and what is involved in making decisions, he should be helped to transfer this learning to a similar situation either in the same or in a different group. Since group work is concerned with the utilization of the decision-making process for purposes of helping individual members achieve goals for themselves, i.e., meeting their own needs as well as contributing to achieving the goals of the group, it follows that group work's interest in decision-making is related to its concern for the enhancement of social functioning of individual group members. Since social functioning means "the sum of the roles performed by a person",[2] group work, as a method of social work, is concerned with helping individual group members enhance their role performances. Decision-making is inherent in any social role which a person is called upon to perform.

Steps and Methods in Decision-Making

Grace Coyle[3] lists four basic steps in decision-making:

1. "Becoming aware of the problem". This includes a definition of the problem and breaking it down into component parts.
2. "Clarifying and evaluating proposed solutions". Delineating the alternatives available and evaluating the possible consequences.
3. "Reaching a decision". Choosing one alternative to the exclusion of others and evaluating the choice as to probable consequences.

---

[2] Boehm, Werner. *Curriculum Study of Council on Social Work Education,* Vol. I, 1961.
[3] Coyle, Grace L. "Concepts Relevant to Helping the Family as a Group", in *Social Casework,* Vol. 43, No. 7 (1962), p. 353.

4. "Acting upon the decision that has been reached". Implementing the decision and evaluating the choice.

I would like to add a *fifth* step here.

Examining the results of implementing the decision.

The consequences of a decision require examination since they may be (and often are) quite unanticipated. What was intended may not bear much resemblance to the actual result. For instance, a street corner group may have decided to stage a rumble anticipating victory over the rival gang; the fight, however, ends with their defeat and in addition to other unanticipated consequences one of their members gets very badly hurt.

These five steps do not necessarily occur in this sequential order. They merely indicate a process which is inherent in decision-making when one begins to analyze its component phases. In group work, we have tended to value more the process of desicion-making than the actual content of the decision itself, although we are not, nor should we be, oblivious to the substance as the brief illustration of the street corner group indicates. Now let me illustrate these steps with an example.

A boys' group may want to invite a girls' group to a party; they have to become aware of the situation, what is involved in this proposal (Step 1); this leads to deliberation, discussion, thinking together, getting ideas on the table, trying them out, rejecting some, accepting others (whom shall we invite, why this group and not any other, etc.) (Step 2). These two steps can be referred to as a "period of anticipation", in which various factors are weighed and evaluated against the frame of reference of the group. Subsequently, a decision is reached. In our example, the group members have made a choice: to invite or not invite the girls' club (Step 3). Depending on the type of decision, the group now acts upon it. If they decided not to invite the girls, the party will not be as some had visualized it and certain consequences will appear within the group. If they decide to invite the club, a "period of implementation" begins. Certain steps have to be taken (the girls have to be notified, new problems have to be anticipated. They may decline to come). A group needs also an opportunity to evaluate its decisions and to have avenues open to change them (Step 4). New evidence may have come to light which puts the decision into a new perspective; the emotional climate of a group may have changed and the decision made at one time may need revision. There is no virtue in sticking to a decision for the sake of sticking to it. The girls have been invited and the party was successful. The group discusses this at their next meeting and get a sense of accomplishment (Step 5).

This illustration is oversimplified and it merely summarizes basic steps. Group life is dynamic, however, and decision-making is complicated by the interpersonal relationships, the group structure and individual need dispositions of members.

To make the situation more lifelike and thereby complicating matters a bit, let us just add that one of the boys has a crush on one of the girls from the club to be invited; another boy has had a longstanding feud with another girl. Undoubtedly, these variables influence the results of the decision. If these boys are high-ranking members of the group, they will be able to influence the others sufficiently to affect the choice one way or the others. (Interpersonal relations in intergroup activity is a subject which has not received a great deal of attention in small group research. See Hare, (1962), Chapters 6 and 7).

Decision-making involves proposals and securing agreement; it involves a power dimension, because some group members may want to control others (and these others in turn may allow themselves to be controlled) in order to get agreement on a decision. If all group members share a set of norms, it is easier to arrive at a decision, providing information as to the possible alternatives and their consequences is sufficient. If a group does not share common norms, the process of decision-making becomes prolonged, since the activity of the group is directed towards securing common norms, towards assuming power rather than towards making a specific decision. "Why do they take so long, why can't they agree, why do they talk around the subject instead of making a decision?" A group worker knows that his first task is to find out "where the group is", e.g., whether the members have common norms and what these are, before the decision-making process can flow. It follows that the worker's task has to be directed towards helping a group to resolve the struggle for common norms before he can help them in reaching decisions in a meaningful way.

This leads to a consideration of the fact that inherent in the decision-making process is conflict, a group phenomenon characterized by tensions and filled with emotions.

113

Decision-making and Conflict[4]

Wilson and Ryland (1950), borrowing from Eubank, describe five categories of conflict-resolution, which can also be utilized for describing methods of decision-making. (op. cit., p. 52).

1. *Elimination:* Individuals and/or sub-groups who disagree with the premises, the nature of the decision, method for reaching it, or the implementation, are "eliminated".

2. *Subjugation:* Here members or sub-groups are forced to submit to a dominant person or sub-group. They are "made to come along". In both categories the actual or potential use of power is implied or stated.

3. *Compromise:* Negotiations take place among different members or sub-groups. Both parties give up something in order to get something else in return. It is essentially a bargaining approach in which costs and rewards are weighed and eventually balanced. Depending on the nature of the balance, some party may feel that the price paid was not worth the reward.

4. *Alliances:* Individuals form into sub-groups and form alliances within a group, with other groups, or with members of other groups. Common interests, values, ideas of people and groups lead them to join others in an attempt to convince those who are on the outside that they had better see the light and follow them. Implied here is a show of strength in numbers and by inference a conviction that this strength is unassailable.

5. *Integration:* Solutions are arrived at that satisfy each member; every one will commot himself and come away feeling satisfied. (Whether this highest level of conflict resolution is always completely achievable is debatable).

With the exception of integration, all other categories of conflict-resolution, in turn, may generate the seed of new conflict. The eliminated resentfully may stage a comeback, the subjected may attempt to become dominant and subjugate the erstwhile victors, those who think they have paid too high a price for the rewards gained may open up the barter agreement and those who have joined one set of alliances may find these alliances no longer valid and desert them in favor of new forces which they may want to bring into being.

---

[4] See Bernstein, Saul. "Conflict in Group Work", the preceding article in this book.

114

It should be kept in mind that there are both verbal and non-verbal means of employing these methods. Physical violence, threatening as well as non-threatening gestures, deliberations, are all in the service of these methods of conflict resolution during the process of decision-making. Drawing lots or tossing a coin as arbiters have not been limited to youth groups. In our culture, we have a distinctive preference about ways of handling conflicts. We place a high value on verbal means (reasoning-out), on compromise and on integration. We chalk up a mark of achievement when group members move from the use of physical force or chance-method to deliberative discussion.

Sub-Cultural Patterns

Sub-cultural behavior patterns are often in direct conflict with deliberate preconceived ideas and values of the dominant culture. In lower-class culture, chance decisions and physical handling are much more an accepted way of solving problems than in a middle-class group.[5] To expect such a group to reason out differing viewpoints could hardly reveal diagnostic astuteness on the part of the worker. Helping such a group to come to terms with the outcome of their methods is probably a major activity of a group worker for a long time, and the goal would be achieved if members become more aware of the consequences as well as of the existence of other ways of making decisions.

Henry Maas[6] writes that the more privileged youth seem to be better prepared to meet expectations for self-directive involvements of democratic planning and decision-making than members of clubs in underprivileged neighborhood centers. He further states: "One suspects — although the research did not pursue this question — that if the group worker had prematurely pushed democratic decision-making on these slum area youngsters, one of two things would have happened. They would have gone off in directions unacceptable to the policies of the community center and/or have left the agency." (Ibid.)

---

[5] See e.g. Miller, Walter B., "Implications of Lower Class Culture for Social Workers", *Social Service Review,* Vol. 3, no. 3, September, 1959, pp. 219–236, and Loeb, Martin R., "Social Class and the American Social System", *Social Work,* Vol. 6, no. 2, April, 1961, pp. 12–18.

[6] Maas, Henry, "Group Influences on Client-Worker Interaction", *Social Work,* Vol. 9, no. 2, April, 1964, p. 74.

This observation is particularly relevant for many of our so-called "alienated" youth groups. They have learned through bitter experience that their range of decision-making is severely limited. Society has put barriers in the way of lower-class youngsters which make it very difficult indeed to develop a feeling that they have a choice about jobs, education, recreation, etc. Maybe that is why they have become alienated and make the kinds of choices which they know they can make regardless of the consequences to themselves and others. As Bernstein (1964) puts it: ". . . so that these youngsters can learn to respect others and to develop what is the right of all people, the opportunity to make intelligent decisions, and to be ready to live with their consequences". (p. 57).

Conversely, a very sophisticated middle-class group might learn that ritualistic vote-taking and Robert's rules of order are not the only means to secure a decision. Many middle-class groups have a tendency to be "ritualistic-oriented". That is, they frequently tend to concentrate heavily on the form of decision-making without taking into account the nature of the process. For example, a group of people may utilize parliamentary procedure regardless of the need for it. Many adolescent groups in middle-class organizations tend to make a fetish out of voting *per se* without being concerned with the substance of the arguments or with the feeling of the members. A group of five members does not require a complex set of Robert's rules of order to arrive at a decision whether to go to a picnic on Saturday or on Sunday. Preoccupation with ritual has displaced concern for dealing with the task efficiently or with helping members to find outlets for their socio-emotional needs. The ritual may have served its purpose at one time at one stage of the group's life; it may no longer be functional now. The ritual has become an end in itself. Functional displacement has occurred.

In group work practice, we frequently see that decisions are arrived at by using all five methods of resolving conflicts in any one group meeting, although a group may move towards employing one of these methods more than any of the others. This depends on the level of group development, the need dispositions of the individual members. and the nature and importance of the decision. Let us turn now to consider each of these in some detail.

Stages of Group Development and Decision-making

Interest in stages or phases of group development has increased in the last few years of small group theory-building and research. In

116

addition to "system-models", "developmental models" have found ready acceptance in small-group theory and group work practice. This theory can be summarized as follows: Change and growth in groups is assumed to occur constantly and is built into the organism of the group itself. Therefore, Phases (stages) occur, and re-occur, and the particular stage of a group is significant not only for its own development, but for those who intervene in the life of the group, e.g., the group worker. Bennis (1962), Thelen, Schutz have become identified with this theoretical orientation. Garland, Kolodny, and Jones have constructed a model for stages of development in social group work groups.[7]

Five general phases — pre-affiliation, power and control, intimacy, differentiation and separation — have been identified and conceptualized by them. States generally occur and re-occur throughout group life, but the dominant aspects of each phase (e.g., "approach-avoidance" issues during the pre-affiliative phase) achieve greater prominence in one phase and the members' needs activated during such a phase require greater attention (e.g. handling their anxieties about being in the group). According to Garland *et al.*, the stage of group development is an important diagnostic determinant for the group worker's intervention.

Since decision-making in all groups is a recurring phenomenon throughout the life span of a group, it follows that the stage models of group development have implications for the decision-making process. Following the Garland-Kolodny-Jones model, we can attempt to identify briefly the nature of decision-making in group work groups during the various stages of their development. Only a sketch reference can be attempted here.

Stage One: During the pre-affiliative phase, group members are making their first adjustment to being in the group, or perhaps stated differently, to being in interaction with other individuals. For the group worker this phase is of major concern since he meets the group where it is and finds it often in the process of initial formation towards structuring itself and of establishing its identity as a group.

Since approach-avoidance problems are dominant and the group tends to avoid the very act of commitment to early decision-making, there is a tentative quality about it. Members tend to model themselves after familiar experiences. "Members draw upon those past experiences which appear similar to the present one".

---

[7] Garland, Kolodny, Jones. *A Model of Stages in Development of Social Group Work Groups,* see second article in this book.

Many social work groups in this early stage typically resemble other types of "Societal" groups, e.g., the scout troop, the Sunday school class, etc. although the particular type of social work group has bearing up on the behavior manifestations, e.g., treatment-oriented groups will show somewhat different patterns from recreational-type groups. However, the referent will tend to be the "non-familial" and "non-intimate" group. Consequently, decision-making will tend to be patterned after those experiences which serve as this frame of reference. Formalistic ritual, such as voting with elaborate procedures, seems to be used with greater frequency. At the same time, it will not be uncommon for many group members (even adults) to rescind their votes at a subsequent meeting and to start their decision-making processes all over again.

Stage Two: It is during phase two in the model when power and control issues are a key theme, that decision-making takes on a most significant aspect in the life of a group and when a foundation can be laid for helping the group to develop decision-making patterns which last into other stages and which can become durable foundations for subsequent choice-making. For this reason, stage two has particular importance for understanding the decision-making process and deserves further elaboration here.

Decision-making and the Power and Control Stage

Schutz (1962) differentiates three interpersonal phases, (1) inclusion, (2) control, and (3) affection. "After the problems of inclusion have been sufficiently resolved, control problems become prominent". Once members are fairly well established in being together in a group, the issue of decision-making arises. This involves problems of sharing responsibility and its necessary concomitant: distribution of power and control. (Op. cit., pp. 3 and 4).[8]

Once a group has solved the problem of inclusion, at least satisfactorily to most members (the approach-avoidance pattern in the Garland *et al.* model) and the members have decided that it is worthwhile to make a preliminary investment in the group, and to stick with it, group structures begin to emerge characterized by the need for predictability on the part of the group members on the one hand, and the need for getting things done for the group-as-a-whole, on the other.

---

[8] Schutz's stage delineations are not basically very different from Garland *et al.* He collapses them into three phases and he does not develop them for purposes of group intervention.

As we have seen in stage one, there are a number of decisions to be made; e.g., the group may have to decide whether to meet again, when to meet, what to do, etc. During this stage, a group is more preoccupied with making an aggregate of individuals into a group, with developing a cohesive identity, and consequently the members are more concerned with testing one another, with handling their anxieties and with their feelings of being included. One could chart stage one and stage two on a continuum-dimension which runs from occupation with self to occupation with others. During stage one, the group member is primarily concerned with issues affecting his self; he is not yet ready to invest too much in others. Decisions are more self-oriented. "What is in it for me?" During stage two, there is a transitional mood. Decisions are viewed by the individual in the light of their impact on others and vice versa. "Will I influence John?" "Will I get Ruth to vote with me?" "Will my siding with Paul affect the outcome of the group's choice to go swimming?"

In stage two, then, characteristic behavior has to do with authority relationships (the worker is a symbol of authority) and interpersonal power dimensions, e.g., who influences whom, who reaches the decisions, who abides by them, etc. The group worker has the opportunity to help the group and its members in the resolution of these conflicts and to help them meet the tasks or problems of this stage. The way in which a group resolves its control struggles through the decision-making process in this phase will determine the ability of the group as a whole to concern itself with the affectional stage, to become emotionally integrated with one another. It will also determine what the individual member has learned in relation to decision-making in a collective situation and how his self-image is affected.

Garland *et al.* suggest three basic issues which need resolution during the "power and control" stage: (1) Rebellion and autonomy relative to their relationship to one another and the group worker; how far can members rebel and yet find protection? (2) Permissive and normative shock; to what extent can members balance non-punitive attitudes and action by the worker with their need for having group norms abided by? Norms afford security; they state what kind of behavior is expected. Violations of norms usually incur punishment. If the worker is non-punitive, how dependable is he in other respects when expected worker-behavior is contrary to group members expectations? (3) Protection and support; this is the period when the group can be either a threat or a refuge. In order to afford support, the group members need assurances that the worker can and will provide them with it in spite of the continuous potential of threat and attack.

Since during this stage, decision making takes on the form of a "power and control struggle", members need assurances that they have a right to make decisions (autonomy) and that this right is safeguarded by the worker. They need a testing laboratory for themselves — an arena for experiencing decision-making, on the one hand, and an arena for resolving the power and control struggle to prepare themselves for the next phase of intimacy, on the other. Therefore, a group member needs to feel that the other members understand him, his position and his feelings around particular issues. In decision-making, a member must have a chance to express his feelings, to bring out his reasoning for or against an issue. A group worker's role is to sense a member's feelings and his position on an issue, to offer him an opportunity to react to it so that he is enabled to deal with the feelings surrounding the issue.

Groups at early stages frequently tend to exhibit impulsive behavior and to pattern their decisions accordingly.

> In an adolescent boys' group, a few of the strongest boys tended to formulate new rules during their meetings in order to gratify their autocratic impulses. If a member of the group got out of line, they would dismiss him or threaten him with expulsion. The worker constantly raised questions which in turn forced the boys to examine their own procedures. Early in the meetings of this group, the club president announced that some of the members had made a new rule about absences of three members whom they wanted to penalize, and they proceeded to invoke these new rules. The worker intervened and helped them see that they could not create a new rule impulsively to fit one or a few members who displeased them without discussing the procedure and applying it to all members. The club president agreed and wanted to rescind this new rule right away; another impulsive act! The worker interpreted this and helped them clarify how decisions have to be considered and arrived at. By pointing out the need for fairness to all, by helping them to air their feelings freely, by examining alternatives, the

members were helped to discover new (if not more satis-fying) ways to relate to each other.

Groups undergo struggles between impulsive and more deliber-ate behavior in all stages, yet, it is in the early stages when the ten-dency to give in to impulsive choice-making is greater and when the group worker's diagnostic alertness and intervention skill can be most helpful to assure impulse control. If we want a group to learn how to transfer the learnings of decision-making, we have to re-interpret continuously and to clarify what has happened in previous situations during the beginning stages of group life. The very nature of bringing about any particular decision may not be in the best interest of all group members, the worker should provide oppor-tunity to open up the channels of communication so that the group can modify its decisions.

Since being included in the group is still of paramount import-ance to a group member, the tendency to use feelings as a basis for decision-making is greater here than at later stages of a group's development, although it is probably never absent. Alliances are formed not because the issues warrant them, but because somebody who has proposed something is liked or disliked. The following interaction process illustrates this point.

Paul was disliked by Kent, Roger, and Chris. He was liked by Ruby, John, and Gary.

Paul: Let's go swimming next week.

Kent: Shut up.

Ruby: Yes, let's — (go swimming.)

Gary: I know where the Y pool is.

Chris: We don't want no pool — we don't want any swimming.

Roger: No — not now — let's go to the movies —

Chris: Terrific. We can all go. How about it, Eddy? (worker)

Worker: wants to say something — is interrupted by *Roger.* Yea, we'll all go to the movies, and that's it.

Paul: I don't want to go —

Kent: I don't want to go, either.

Worker: Now let's look at both suggestions —

Roger: (Interrupts) Paul, you are a stinker. Your stupid ideas —

Gary:	Stupid — we go to the movies and that's it.
Worker:	There are two ideas about our special trip next week. Let me discuss each one.
Paul:	Yea, let's —
Chris:	Only, if we go to the movies.
John:	I go swimming with Paul and that's that.
Worker:	I said, let's discuss *both* ideas.
Paul:	Go ahead.
Kent:	Roger — what d'you say?
Roger:	Let's listen to Eddy. I am with Christ. Quiet.
Worker:	We can do both, but not at the same time. I have a suggestion; let's see what we can do about going to the movies *and* going swimming. There are even other things we can do together . . .

The boys essentially would have just as well gone swimming as to the movies. Their arguments were not rational. They were based on their respective likes and dislikes. It was up to the worker to have the group accept a more rational base for decision-making and to minimize the emotional grounds for choosing alternatives.

In this stage, the group worker is actively participating in the decision-making process. While a group worker does not make a decision *for* a group, he will assume a more deliberate role in pointing out more actively the alternatives and consequences of action than at a later stage when the group has increased its capacity to contribute decisions on grounds of rational thinking through group deliberation. The decision-making process, however, should not become an end in itself. Some groups have developed it into a fetish, and ends have become the means, the form has become a substitute for substance. Of importance for the group worker at this stage is the recognition that each member is concerned with his position in the group, his influence, and his role. Primary anxieties evolve around having too much of too little influence. Every member wants to be comfortable with the next person and wants to feel that his needs are adequately met in and through the group.

Having dwelt on this stage which is so crucial for the decision-making process, let me now sketch very briefly decision-making in relation to the other three stages.

Stage Three: Once a group achieves a degree of mastery of the tasks posed by the power and control struggle through decision-

122

making processes, it may be ready to move towards the next step in the developmental model which Garland *et al.* call "intimacy" and which uses the family as a frame of reference. Since this phase is characterized by a greater degree of personal involvement and other-orientation, decision-making patterns manifest a stronger show of emotions. Members' relationships are more cohesive and their decision-making has a ring of intimacy. They use more informal procedures, often characterized by quick assent and quick dissent. Decisions are made with greater emotional investments; love and hate motifs are underlying qualities of the decisions. This, of course, assumes that their power struggle at stage two has been sufficiently resolved to allow the freer give and take essential to making choices. The group has assumed now a great deal of meaning to the members as an entity and decisions are seen against this perspective of meaningfulness. Therefore, the consequences of a decision are seen by members in the light of its significance to *their* group. The group worker here must clarify not only inter-personal feelings, but the way in which the members' choice-making affects the group-as-a-whole.

Stage Four: The group members are ready to accept one another as distinct individuals within the distinctive group, all of their own. Mutual support is becoming evident. Decision-making now tends to become more rational; group members have their choices or more objective data available to them, or they tend to look for facts upon which to base the decision.

It is during this stage that the goal of minimizing the *non-*rational elements in decision making can be best achieved, since the earlier inter-personal conflicts have been resolved to an appreciable degree. Now groups may be more ready to "run themselves". The group worker can encourage the group to make decisions on their own with his role more confined to being a resource person.

Stage Five: This stage signals the completion of the group experience with its attendant regression patterns. This may be reflected in decision-making characteristics reminiscent of stages one, two, and three. The worker's intervention, focused on facilitating evaluation and on building bridges to the future, must concern itself with giving support to group members' choice-making, with sorting out the pro's and con's of a decision and with concentrating on the rational aspects of the consequences. Decisions will affect the member's future either in another group or in a new social role. The degree to which they have internalized the methods of making decisions in this group will be a valuable foundation for the future. This is the stage in which the worker needs to help buttress learned behavior and link it to the future of the individuals.

Need Dispositions of Members and Decision-making

Not only the developmental level of the group, but also that of levels of individual members are of importance. Diagnostic considerations in group work make it imperative to look at the need dispositions and developmental tasks. The literature is not very informative about how various age groups perceive choice-making or what meaning the choice-process has for different age groups.

Group work practice has been mostly concerned with the following four gross-age-groupings: latency, adolescence, adults, and older adults. Let us briefly look at these now.

Latency-age children tend to be more impulsive, move influenced by their emotional tendencies and affective thinking. The culture of the elementary school with its accepting authority patterns prevails as a model for the latency child. Choices are circumscribed by the power of adult authority. Decision-making is modelled after their experience with authorities in the home and in the school. Therefore, a group service agency assumes a major role in broadening the horizon of the youngster, in offering him an opportunity to test himself in the arena of decision-making with his peers, guided by the influence of the worker's authority.

The turbulence of *adolescence* tends to aggravate the confusion involved in making choices. Adolescents, particularly, are faced with making pretty difficult decisions, notably in two major areas of their lives: search for a mate and search for a vocation. The seriousness of the long-term consequences of these decisions at a time of biological, social, and emotional turmoil distinguishes this life period from any other. Making decisions for the sake of completing a task becomes a predominant theme in teenage groups. Consequently, they need opportunities to test out decisions, to become attuned to the ingredients of choice-making, and to learn to anticipate consequences and live with them with responsibility, while receiving support from the group worker. The upheavals of adolescence are reflected in the nature and methods of decision-

124

making. What an individual youngster experiences during adolescence flows into his participation in making group decisions. Many a group worker with adolescents recalls the experience of group members rescinding their decisions at which they have elaborately arrived. For weeks a group may deliberate and decide to buy jackets or to sponsor a dance; all details have been carefully worked out. At a meeting during the following week, the group hardly remembers that any of these decisions had been made.

While it may be assumed that *adult groups* experience rational and mature levels of decision making, we have enough evidence to question this assumption. Developmentally speaking, adults are expected to function in many roles which require decision-making capacities and experiences, and many adults participate in task-oriented groups in which decision-making is the *sine qua non* of their existence. These experiences can have positive and negative effects upon adult group members depending upon the way they are structured and utilized. Since many such groups have an impact upon community life (e.g., civic groups) the decision-making processes used deserve close attention and analysis. Group workers have not only an opportunity, but also a responsibility to assist in this process both for the individual concerned and for the outcome of the group's goals.

Many *older adults* in our society have become deprived of their decision-making functions, a most significant loss. Their contributions are not sought after, their own field of choice-making is circumscribed and their life-field is shrinking. It follows that meaningful choice-making needs to be given increased attention, to help them to maintain their self-respect and to give them a continued sense of self-worth. Too many group work experiences with the aged exist in a world of make-believe since many of the choices which they are offered are not real and meaningful.[9]

The world of older people has been contracting. Many status and role changes have occurred for them, e.g., they find themselves in non-work roles, their former group affiliations have often been dissolved, their circle of friends and acquaintances has diminished and quite a few older people are faced with the task of "re-socialization". They have to establish new relationships with

---

[9] See, for example, Lowy, Louis, "Meeting the Needs of Older People on a Differential Basis", *Social Group Work with Older People,* Lake Mohawk, 1963, and Kubie, S. and Landau, G., *Group Work with the Aged,* International Universities Press, 1954 (especially Chapter 3).

contemporaries and find new modes of adapting to unaccustomed roles, such as grandparents, retirees, etc. While their choice-opportunities are diminishing, they are expected to make choices among alternatives of which they have little knowledge.

One could say that choice opportunities increase in scope during adolescence and decrease in scope with senescence. In work with older adults, the group worker has to be aware of these factors and offer older people realistic experiences in choice-making to assist them in maintaining previously learned skills in decision-making and to apply these to their new life situation. An older person may be helped a great deal by recognizing that his vote in a self-governing older adult group has significance, that he was able to influence the outcome of an election in his group. This may become a bridge to other ventures in decision-making which may affect his future life and his self-image, despite the fact that many previously available choice alternatives have been curtailed.[9]

Taking into account this overwhelming complexity of need dispositions and developmental tasks at different age levels, a few *generalizations* can be drawn.

1. Each group member's self-image is affected by a variety of experiences, many of which are beyond the control of group work. But the way an individual's contribution to the decision-making process is handled by the group worker will have impact upon the self-image of the person and will contribute to developing a sense of autonomy by encouraging him to make a contribution to the solution of a problem with which the group is struggling. The worker uses techniques of support of individual members and helps them to clarify what has happened in the situation. This is exemplified with older adults who often have lost a great deal of their sense of autonomy. In participating in making choices and in seeing the results of their choices, the worker can make a contribution toward enhancing their sense of autonomy. In many instances, people have a faulty reality perception. This is generally more true of adolescents, when their sense of identity has not yet crystallized. Decision-making opportunities can help them in some measure to get a clearer perception of reality by experiencing consciously the consequences of their decisions.

2. While the group meeting *per se* offers an opportunity for decision-making, it is often outside the group that an individual makes decisions pertaining to the group, e.g., whether to continue

in the group, whether to carry out the assignments that were given to him, etc. It may happen that a sub-group was formed to accomplish a task which the group had delegated. It is frequently difficult for individual members to carry out these assigned tasks without proper guidance. The worker will meet with a sub-group separately and point out how their decision-making process will influence the implementation of the larger decision that was made by the group as a whole. Or there may be one or two members who find it difficult to relate in the sub-group; they may feel threatened. The worker will work individually with the members to show how their participation can help resolve the issues in the larger group and how they can gain greater acceptance.

3. Many program activities can be so structured that decision-making becomes part of them. Since groups afford individuals an opportunity to perform in roles which are group created, we can assume that many are decision-making roles and that group members are initiating as well as implementing and evaluating decisions. Depending on the nature of the group and individual characteristics, some members seem to be more in the role of initiators of decisions while others are more in those of implementing and evaluating decisions. For some members, it may be more difficult to change their roles, but it is the group worker's task to make varied experiences available to them, based on the diagnosis of the group and its members.

4. Members learn not only to adapt to group needs but also to change group goals and group norms, and to transfer the learning gained to new situations. For this reason, the worker tries to make available repeated opportunities for practising skills learned in decision-making and for articulating feelings about them. At the beginning stages, the worker has to be very supportive so that the decisions made are not only realistic and produce a minimum of frustration but that they set the tone for the group as a whole to build subsequent decisions on firmer foundations, which in turn will contribute to better functioning of the group as a whole and its individual members.

5. Related to age-level developmental tasks is the range of significance of the content of the decision. At each age level, the appropriateness of the content of the decision can be taken as an index of maturity. For instance, middle-class adolescent boys and girls who are concerned with dating, selection of a vocational

127

career, latest musical fads, sports, etc., appropriately would reflect these concerns in group meetings and choices would focus around these matters. If a group of middle-class adolescents were to remain concerned only about musical fads and in their life together would never engage in grappling with vocational choices, with relationships to members of the same and opposite sex or with public issues of the day, a group worker would consider it his responsibility to stimulate this group to increase their repertoire of group activities and therefore to open up wider vistas for decision making.

A group worker with street corner boys will want to engage these boys in relating their group experiences to matters of personal significance. Bernstein (1964) comments, "Problems such as those in school, jobs, relationships with the police, their minority status, sex, and other subjects vital to their lives are important possibilities for discussions as the group is ready for them . . ." And further, he says, "An important concomitant accomplishment could be the fostering of the youth's ability to verbalize and discuss problems and solutions. They are often impatient with this kind of talk; yet the ability to put such matters clearly, to listen to what others say about them, and to stay with the issues long enough to achieve movement are essential skills for mature adulthood." (p. 102).

The group worker has a responsibility to structure decision-making experiences which would move the content from the less significant (in their terms) to the more significant.

Nature and Importance of the Decision

In addition to the level of group development and need dispositions of individual members, the nature of the decision itself is a significant variable. It does make a difference whether the group makes a decision whether to meet again or to break up or whether to choose between using green or blue paint on a wall-mural for the Settlement House Christmas party. In addition to individual desires, interests, and needs, several group properties influence the nature of the decision, notably group activities, group goals, and group cohesiveness. What the group does at a particular moment has a bearing upon the kinds of decisions which are apt to be made. A group engaged in planning a party will be involved in decisions about timing, program, refreshments, etc. A group which has as its goal the setting up of a self-governing structure in the ward of a hospital will be concerned with deciding upon the type of self-government, the people who will be elected to various positions and so forth. A group which has developed a strong "we-feeling" will not be concerned with deciding whether to remain together as a group.

The degree of investment which the members have in the group as a whole, in the nature of the decision, and in the consequences of the decision is another important aspect of decision-making. When tightly knit group X is about to make a decision about the timing of a camping trip, members will take into consideration their own time schedule. If the group proposes Saturday and Johnny knows he has to help his father in his store on that day, Johnny will be influenced by this knowledge. The degree of importance of the decision to individuals and to the group requires careful assessment on the part of the group worker since choice-making and implementation will be heavily affected by this variable. Since group decisions require varying degrees of accommodations of members for the benefit of the whole group, their readiness and willingness to subordinate personal investment to group interest demands sensitive understanding and skilful guidance by the group worker.

Intervention of the Social Group Worker

It may be useful to conclude with a brief summarization of some intervention approaches which the social group worker should utilize in order to harness the natural decision-making process in small groups to the service of his goals as a helping agent. It is primarily through the group worker's interventive skills that decision-making can be utilized for helping purposes.

Like all social workers, the group worker is engaged in exploration (study), diagnosis and treatment. He is concerned with the following components: community, agency, group, individual member, program media (tools), and himself as a worker. He has values and attitudes; he has goals derived from his professional and agency identification. He uses knowledge and understanding of these components and brings to bear his skills acquired through training and experience.

What interventive approaches does a group worker use to help a group in the decision-making process?

1. He helps the group determine whether there is only one issue or several. If there are several, they have to be broken down

129

into workable units, so that primary issues may be decided first. As Alan Klein (1962) says, "At the onset, the worker helps the group clarify the issues so that members are agreed on the problem about which they are about to make a decision. The problem must be worded clearly in terms about which there is no disagreement or ambiguity. This avoids prolonged discussion which results in a final realization that everyone meant the same thing but used different terminology, or that the terms used meant different things to different people." (p. 56).

The worker now helps the group look for tentative solutions. There may be two or three or a dozen. If there are a dozen possibilities and the group can think of only two, the worker should ask questions to open new vistas, pointing out or leading to new horizons. After having elicited all he can from the group, he may then have to say, "Have you thought of this?" "What do you think of that?" In this sense, the worker acts as a catalyst who brings to bear his resources, knowledge and experience, the facts, and above all, a change to open up new vistas which may have escaped the group because they are very much involved in an emotional turmoil or because they do not know about them.

Since decision-making is a "clarification process", a sorting out of possible alternatives with an anticipation of consequences, the group worker has a clarifying and interpretative function utilizing techniques of support to maintain the interest of the group. For example, a group may discuss whether they should meet on Wednesday or Thursday the following week. The worker will help them sort out the advantages and disadvantages of either day; he may point out the availability of the agency and of his time and ask them whether they have any preferences or any previous commitments. In this process, he begins to use his relationship with the group members and eventually they will accept the worker as a person who can help them sort out the various issues involved and clarify the reasons for alternatives. Later on, the worker will want to refer back to similar experiences in decision-making when the issues become more complicated and when the anticipated consequences are not as apparent. Although the group may have decided to meet Thursday instead of Wednesday, there may be certain unanticipated factors which may prevent them from meeting, such as bad weather conditions. This should show them that some consequences of decision-making cannot be anticipated, that there are limits to rational decision-making.

If the individual members have invested a great deal of themselves in the outcome of a decision, then feelings will become more overriding and the nature of the decision will be influenced by emotions. The worker helps a group learn that decisions *cannot* always be rational.

2. Group life affords an opportunity to learn that in the decision-making process not everybody's wishes, desires and needs can be fulfilled. Let us return to our example of the party. They all agreed to have a dance, but there is conflict as to the type of dance, whom to invite, etc. Some resolution of this conflict will have to be found. The methods of resolving this conflict are as important as the specific resolution.

In the enumeration of the methods of conflict resolution, we indicated a hierarchial value preference. And yet, depending on the diagnostic assessment of the group and its members, the worker helps the group in the type of method most appropriate at that time; at the same time, he uses this opportunity to point out that there are other methods available and their advantages and disadvantages. The worker interprets to the group that the outcome of the decision may be less important than the method through which they have arrived at a decision. When we refer to the "democratic method" we essentially mean the readiness of the minority to submit to the decision of the majority but at the same time to provide for safeguards on the rights of the minority. Without this safeguarding of the minority viewpoint in a group, only the tyranny of the majority could be maintained. At the same time, group members have to recognize that the minority must not exercise the tyranny over the majority by manipulating a group decision in such a way that it cannot be implemented.

3. The worker also provides a channel for the group to evaluate decisions made in relation to group life, and offers opportunities to revise a decision when it becomes apparent that the original premises no longer hold true. For example, a group of girls may have decided to perform a play and find that despite all efforts, they cannot obtain a particular script which would have been suitable. A change of this decision towards a different type of script is indicated. Another group may have arrived at a decision to put on a play, but it becomes apparent that they cannot yet work together to assure the kind of performance which had seemed possible to them. Shifting to a different activity is

131

indicated with the worker assuming a re-directive, supportive role. Group factors (lack of integrative capacity) and individual factors (risk of exposure) may have been responsible and would have constituted an ego-destructive experience rather than an ego-enhancing experience.

4. It is important to emphasize again that there are differences among groups. For example, gang groups and groups whose members show pathological symptoms need more control and support. In such groups, all individuals are not equally equipped physically, intellectually, or emotionally to participate in the decision-making process. Some members who are emotionally and/or physically handicapped must be protected from making decisions until they are ready to do so. The worker has a responsibility to protect the whole group from making too many decisions that would lead to failure and for which the members are not ready to assume responsibility. For certain groups and at certain times, it is advisable to avoid making decisions. Groups may have to be helped not to make a choice — to leave alternatives open — to avoid "closure", to keep issues in suspense. The group worker has to assess whether a group and its members are ready for decision-making or whether it is better to leave things open. The worker then helps members not to decide, he supports them in *non*-choice-making or in *non*-implementing a decision that may have adverse effect on the members involved. This may be a most worthwhile experience for quite a few adult groups particularly with a strict middle-class orientation.

A group of parents may find it a relief to get support not to carry out their child-psychology lecture series, when it becomes apparent that the members have difficulty coming to grips with emotional material or when it tends to create anxiety and guilt. Non-implementation here may lead to a new look at the members' needs and their readiness for certain group experiences. If properly guided and supported by the worker, such an experience would be salutory for the group, because they would be able to learn that not carrying out certain decisions can have its own virtues.

5. The members within themselves have resources which the group worker will use in the choice-making process. They have ego-strengths and abilities, knowledge and skills in a wide range of areas. Older adults, for example, have many life experiences which can be called upon to give a sense of wisdom and balance to decision making. When a group of older people is in the process

132

of deciding whether to support a rally for "Medicare", their personal experiences with health problems, their know-how in communicating these experiences to others, their skill in presenting the issues which many of them had acquired in labor unions, are invaluable resources on which the group worker will want to build. It is the emphasis on strengths of group members which characterizes so much of the group worker's interventive activities, whether they are directed towards older adults, middle-class children, or lower-class adolescents.

6. Since decisions are based on facts, ideas, and values, the group worker's roles which include the functions of information giving and a bearer of values, are of significance in the decision-making process. Knowledge of facts (both as basis of decisions and for their consequences) and awareness of values are essential. While emotional and unconscious factors interfere with rational decision-making, the group worker has to be ready to supply information to the group members which can be utilized by the group to make a cognitive choice.

At the same time, the worker's skill in sorting out the group's values is important so that the members may become aware of the reasons for their choices:

A group of older adults wanted to plan a New Year's Eve Party. When making this decision, they indicated that they thought this would not entail many preparations and the party could be planned with a minimum of problems. They were getting quite worked up and started planning with a good deal of gusto. The worker knew that their adult children had traditionally relied on many of these group members to be their baby sitters on New Year's Eve. He was aware that many of these grandparents had been ambivalent about this arrangement. Before they were to make a decision (which could have many consequences beyond the immediate party), the group members had to be reminded of the facts. The worker recalled for the group members that in previous years they had been baby sitters for their grandchildren and their own children were probably counting on their service again. He pointed out other alternatives for baby sitting arrangements. These facts became part of the decision-making process. The worker also initiated discussions on values in our society about relationships of parents and adult children and the reciprocal feelings involved in such relationships. The members took these factors into account when they were helped to evaluate the attributes and consequences of their decision about a New Year's Party. Before reaching a final decision, they met with their (adult) children as a group utilizing the worker as a catalyst – and reviewed the total situation. Eventually, they arrived at the decision to hold the party. This decision, however, was based on a conscious awareness of the premises for the decision, a sorting-out of various alternatives and a cognitive awareness of the consequences of the decision. Finally, the children of the older adults were included in the decision-making. This broadening of the client system – the older adults – by linking it with a tangential system – their children – led to better communication and enabled the older adults to become comfortable with the consequences of their choice. The worker as a resource person and catalyst was instrumental in this process.

Conclusion

Since one of the major goals of the group worker is the internalization of desired changes in behavior over time, the group worker's intervention relative to decision making will be concerned with helping the members to internalize methods and content of decision making which are:

> Appropriate to the developmental age level of the group members
> appropropriate to the stage of the group's development,
> appropriate to the value system of the social work.

In order to move along the road towards an approximation of this goal, the worker must insure maximum participation of the members in choice-making and to provide opportunities for maximum satisfaction in participating. In order to change old behavior patterns to new ones and to stabilize these changes, people must have a chance to practice new modes of behavior; in so doing, they need to have a sense of worthwhileness and satisfaction. The social group worker has to offer support to the group as a whole and its individual members in and outside the group.

Support as a mode of helping activity is as crucial here as it is in other interventive acts of the worker.[10] Eventually, the group will be moving towards a decreasing need for help from the worker to make mature decisions within the framework which we have just reviewed. Eventually, the members will move towards the separation stage and be ready to use this group experience as a frame of reference, as a jumping-off point for new experiences, for new learning. Hopefully, they learned to apply their past gains for their own satisfaction and for the good of our democratic society which depends for its functioning and indeed survival upon knowledgeable and well informed people who can make intelligent, mature, rational decisions in their various roles, but above all in their role as citizens.

REFERENCES

BALES, ROBERT F., *Interaction Process Analysis,* Addison Wesley Publishing Co., Cambridge, 1950.

BENNE, KENNETH, CHIN, ROBERT and BENNIS, WARREN in *The Planning of Change,* Holt, Rinehardt, and Winston, New York, 1962.

BERNSTEIN, SAUL, "Conflict in Group Work", see preceeding article in this book.

——— *Youth on the Streets,* Association Press, New York, 1964.

BOEHM, WERNER, *Curriculum Study of Council on Social Work Education.,* Vol. I, 1961.

COYLE, GRACE L., "Concepts Relevant to Helping the Family as a Group", *Social Casework,* Vol. 43, No. 7, 1962.

FREY, LOUISE A., "Support and the Group, A Generic Treatment Form", *Social Work,* Vol. 7, No. 4, 1962.

GARLAND, JAMES, KOLODNY, RALPH and JONES, HUBERT, "A Model for Stages of Development in Social Work Groups", see second article in this book.

HARE, PAUL H., *Handbook of Small Group Research,* Free Press, Glencoe, Illinois, 1962.

KLEIN, ALAN, *Society, Democracy, and the Group,* Woman's Press, New York, 1962.

KUBIE, SUSAN and LANDAU, G., *Group Work with the Aged,* International Universities Press, 1954.

---

[10] See for example, Frey, Louise, "Support and the Group, A Generic Treatment Form", *Social Work,* Vol. 7, No. 4, October, 1962, pp. 35–42.

LOEB, MARTIN R., "Social Class and the American Social System", *Social Work,* Vol. 6, No. 2, April, 1961.

LOWY, LOUIS, "Meeting the Needs of Older People on a Differential Basis", *Social Group Work with Older People,* 1963, Lake Mohawk Conference Proceedings.

MAAS, HENRY S., "Group Influences on Client — Worker Interaction", *Social Work,* Vol. 9, No. 2, 1964.

MILLER, WALTER B., "Implications of Lower Class Culture for Social Workers", *Social Service Review,* Vol. 33, No. 3, September, 1959.

SCHUTZ, WILLIAM C., "Interpersonal Underworld", *The Planning of Change* edited by Benne, Bennis, and Chin, Holt, Rinehardt, Winston, New York, 1962.

WASSERMAN, P., and SILANDER, FRED, *Decision-Making, An Annotated Bibliography,* Graduate School of Business in Public Administration, Cornell University, Ithaca, New York, 1958.

WILSON, G., and RYLAND, G., *Social Group Work Practice,* Houghton Mifflin and Co., 1950.